IDOLS
OF THE
MIND

How Systems Shape Our
Thoughts, Beliefs, and Behaviors

Book 1
Systems of Science

Randy M. Herring

Also by Randy M. Herring

The Fitness Mindset: 7 Habits for Peak Performance To Get Strong, Lean, and Fit (2021)

Reflections on Growth: An Existential Journey (2025)

IDOLS
OF THE
MIND

How Systems Shape Our
Thoughts, Beliefs, and Behaviors

Book 1
Systems of Science

By
Randy M. Herring

This four-volume, seven-book work is an exploratory inquiry rather than a declaration of truth. It draws on Francis Bacon's idols of the mind to examine the false mental constructs that distort human thought. The Idols of the Theater, Marketplace, Cave, and Tribe appear here not as historical concepts but as living forces in contemporary life. The ideas presented are offered as tools for examination, not doctrines for belief. Readers are encouraged to question ideas, including those found within these pages. Any meaning derived from this work belongs to the reader alone, along with responsibility for its interpretation and use.

Typeset in New Caledonia, 10.5 and 8.5 point.

Cover design by Randy M. Herring.

This book is part of a larger work consisting of four volumes and seven books.
This is Book 1 of Volume One.

ISBN: 979-8-9950867-1-0

"I do not feel obliged to believe that the same God who has endowed us with senses, reason, and intellect has intended to forgo their use."[1]

Galileo

CONTENTS

Contents (cont'd.)

Contents (cont'd.)

Contents (cont'd.)

IDOLS OF THE MIND

PREFACE

The world is built on systems—structures so deeply woven into our experience that they shape the way we perceive reality. They shape our days, our choices, even our sense of self. We are born into them—not by consent, but by default. They teach us how to speak, how to think, what to value, and what to fear. In time, we forget they were ever constructed.

And yet something lingers—a quiet discomfort, a sense that beneath the surface of routine lies something unspoken. What if the life you call your own was authored before you ever asked who you are? What if the freedom you feel is merely the freedom to choose between paths already laid?

The paradox is this: you are not chained, and still you are not free. The prison is not around you—it is within, crafted from beliefs never questioned and truths never chosen. Systems are not merely external institutions; they become internalized patterns that shape the human mind—its interpretations, values, and sense of identity. In time, the conditioned mind helps preserve the very structures that shaped it.

Systems exist everywhere. Mainstream science determines what is regarded as true. Philosophical ideologies legitimize what is recognized as power. Religious institutions define what is sacred. Educational structures establish which knowledge is valued. Health care organizations decide what is necessary to prevent illness. Agricultural industries regulate what food is classified as safe to eat.

Language sets the boundaries of expression—shaping what is spoken, what is silenced, and how narratives are framed. It carries unspoken assumptions and cultural inheritance, and its meaning is continually reshaped through everyday use.

Identity develops over time through personal experience and social interaction, formed by habits, environments, and institutional expectations. When identity appears fixed, it narrows interpretation, limits growth, and constrains openness to new perspectives.

Human nature is shaped by common cognitive patterns that influence how we interpret the world. These patterns are reinforced through habit and strengthened by social approval and disapproval. Such feedback encourages conformity, often at the expense of awareness and independent judgment.

Together, these systems form a web of influence. When we submit to them, external structures become internalized. Once internalized, they guide our choices and decisions, quietly sustaining the very systems that shape us.

Questioning these systems is often portrayed as destabilizing, while assimilation is framed as offering security and belonging—though at the cost of autonomy. Complete separation from systems is rare, if not impossible, because they provide access to resources tied to basic human needs: food, shelter, safety, employment, and social connection. This interdependence makes detachment impractical.

The effects are not only structural but relational. Relationships with those who operate within or benefit from prevailing systems can create divided loyalties—to individuals and to the structures they represent. This overlap can deepen assimilation and erode self-awareness, sometimes leading to what some describe as a state of "nothingness."[2] These dynamics often unfold unconsciously, particularly within communities guided by respected authority figures.

I have confronted such systems firsthand, as recounted in Books 2, 3, 6, and 7. In my twenties, I belonged to a religious institution grounded in unquestioned belief—one that praised obedience, marginalized dissent, and disciplined those who challenged its doctrine. In my forties, I worked within a business organization shaped by shared assumptions that rewarded compliance over conscience and discouraged scrutiny of inconsistent practices. In my fifties, I taught symbolic logic within a community college system—a subject never previously studied or taught—so a book suited to the way the material could be learned was selected, and a customized edition was created with the publisher before the course began. In my sixties, I participated in jury selection and openly challenged the ideological premises of a judicial system grounded in legitimacy, consensus, and authority—one that often prioritizes ritual over reflection and silences those willing to question its assumptions. In each case, I chose conscience over automatic compliance.

Whether we consciously defend certain systems or unconsciously support them, these frameworks shape our thoughts, beliefs, and behaviors, thereby profoundly influencing our quality of life. What could be more significant than clinging to one or more of these systems? As Aristotle observed, the habits we form early in life are profoundly important, shaping our lives in ways that make all the difference.[3]

True freedom begins when we refuse to be molded—when we choose active thought over passive acceptance.

To help understand how these systems shape the human mind, Francis Bacon's concept of the "idols of the mind" shows how false mental constructs distort human thought. These idols—classed as the Theater, the Marketplace, the Cave, and the Tribe—highlight how authority, language, identity, and human nature become internalized systems that subtly shape our understanding of the world and ourselves.

Idols of the Theater are systems imposed by authority. They distort truth by encouraging uncritical acceptance of dominant epistemic frameworks—science, ideology, religion, education, health care, and agriculture—that present their claims as definitive. These frameworks consolidate power by establishing what counts as legitimate knowledge while suppressing dissent and transforming inquiry into doctrine. By shaping the boundaries of thought, they restrict intellectual freedom and discourage critical examination. To defend this idol is to say, "Trust the experts," rewarding compliance and penalizing dissent.

If the Idols of the Theater establish what may be believed, the Idols of the Marketplace determine how belief is expressed and transmitted.

Idols of the Marketplace are systems shaped by language. They distort meaning through the habitual use of words laden with hidden assumptions, cultural inheritance, and ambiguity. These distortions rest on the illusion that language is neutral and precise. When language goes unexamined, it constrains thought, reinforces power, and reduces complex realities to simplified labels. By determining how ideas are named, framed, and repeated, these systems shape belief and steer behavior. To defend this idol is to say, "Everyone knows what that means," relying on familiarity to manufacture agreement.

Language does not merely structure ways of speaking and thinking—it also shapes the individual who receives them.

Idols of the Cave are systems formed through identity.[4] They distort interpretation by anchoring thought in personal experience—background, habit, education, and environment. These identity-bound filters narrow perspective and generate resistance to ideas that challenge one's worldview. They treat identity as fixed rather than evolving, overlooking how both external forces and internal assumptions continually shape self-understanding. To defend this idol is to say, "This is just who I am," avoiding perspectives that provoke discomfort or transformation.

But even identity rests on something deeper: the innate makeup of human nature.

Idols of the Tribe are systems rooted in human nature.[5] They distort reality through shared cognitive tendencies—pattern-seeking, emotional filtering, social alignment, and the pull of consensus. These mental inclinations draw us toward what feels familiar, affirmed, or collectively endorsed. While they foster belonging and cooperation, they also narrow awareness and weaken independent judgment. By subtly redirecting attention and shaping values—often through repetition and distraction— they amplify conformity without our conscious awareness. To defend this idol is to say, "It is what it is," elevating consensus or comfort above reflection and authenticity.

Together, these idols act as internal filters, shaping the human mind before we become aware of them. If we accept them unquestioningly, we sacrifice both mental and moral clarity, weakening our ability to think freely and act deliberately.

The books that follow, collectively referred to as "the work," *Idols of the Mind,* show how false mental constructs distort human thought through modern systems of conformity, complexity, and repetition. Through philosophical analysis, historical parallels, and contemporary examples, the work demonstrates how consent is manufactured and how conformity gradually comes to be experienced as freedom.

The work is structured as a four-volume, seven-book analysis, with each volume addressing a distinct idol through which systems exert influence:

- **Volume One — Idols of the Theater**
  - Book 1: Systems of Science
  - Book 2: Systems of Ideology
  - Book 3: Systems of Religion and Education
  - Book 4: Systems of Health Care and Agriculture
- **Volume Two — Idols of the Marketplace**
  - Book 5: Systems of Language
- **Volume Three — Idols of the Cave**
  - Book 6: Systems of Identity
- **Volume Four — Idols of the Tribe**
  - Book 7: Systems of Human Nature

Throughout the text, unfamiliar terms are defined at the point of introduction, in subsequent sections, or in explanatory endnotes.

Idols of the Mind: How Systems Shape Our Thoughts, Beliefs, and Behaviors is more than a critique. It is a challenge—a call to examine what you believe, why you believe it, and who benefits from those beliefs.

INTRODUCTION

For much of European history, scientific knowledge was shaped by inherited systems of thought. Even in the sixteenth century, the philosophy of Aristotle (384–322 BCE), developed nearly two millennia earlier, continued to dominate natural inquiry. In *On the Heavens*, Aristotle taught that the Earth stood motionless at the center of the universe, a view known as geocentrism. This model was later refined by Ptolemy (100–170 CE) in the *Almagest*. By the fourth and fifth centuries, this Aristotelian–Ptolemaic framework had been absorbed into Christian theology and education. What began as philosophical speculation became institutionalized doctrine.

Geocentric — "Earth as the Center"

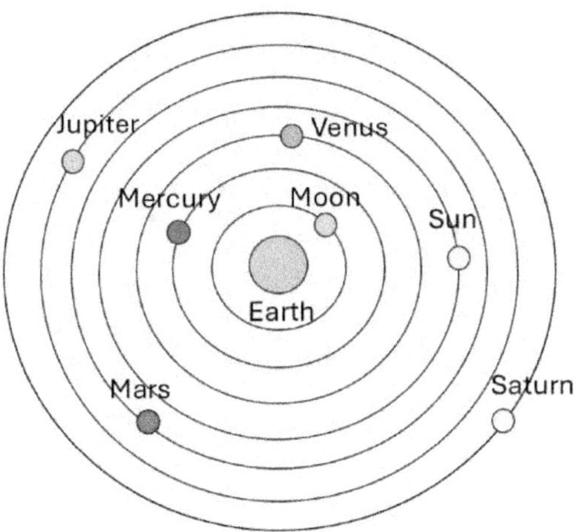

Over time, the geocentric universe was no longer experienced as theory but as common sense—supported by scientific tradition, religious authority, and cultural repetition. It functioned not merely as an explanation of celestial motion but as a system that shaped how reality itself was understood.

The Scientific Revolution (1543–1687) marked a decisive rupture in this inherited order. Thinkers such as Copernicus, Galileo, Descartes, and Bacon challenged long-standing assumptions and transformed how knowledge about the natural world was acquired, justified, and defended.

A pivotal moment came in 1543 with the publication of *On the Revolutions of the Heavenly Spheres* by Nicolaus Copernicus (1473–1543). In proposing a heliocentric model—placing the Sun rather than the Earth at the center—Copernicus did more than revise astronomy. He destabilized a worldview that had been sustained for centuries by institutional authority. Although cautiously presented, his theory implied that humanity was not the center of the universe. The psychological and theological implications were profound.

Heliocentric — "Sun as the Center"

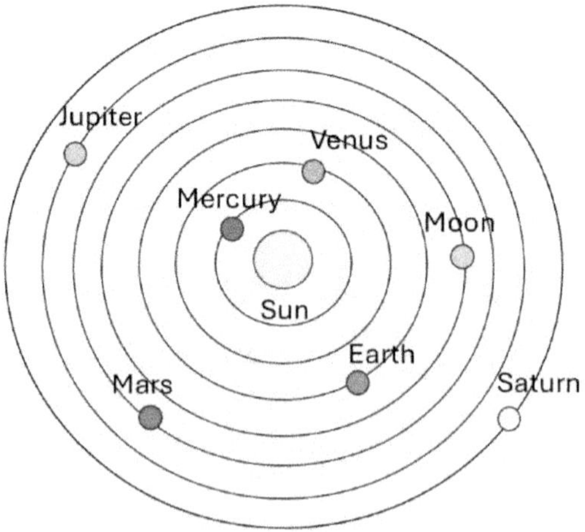

In the early seventeenth century, Galileo Galilei (1564–1642) intensified this challenge. Through telescopic observation, he identified phenomena—such as Jupiter's moons and the phases of Venus—that contradicted geocentrism. In 1632, his *Dialogue Concerning the Two Chief World Systems* openly favored heliocentrism.[6]

The following year, he was tried by the Roman Inquisition, forced to recant, and placed under house arrest. His condemnation symbolized a deeper conflict: not merely between science and religion, but between emerging evidence and entrenched systems of authority. Not until 1992 did the Catholic Church officially acknowledge that Galileo's conclusions were correct.[7]

Galileo's trial reverberated across Europe. René Descartes (1596–1650), having completed his *Treatise on Light* in 1633—which affirmed heliocentrism—nearly destroyed the manuscript after hearing Galileo's condemnation and chose not to publish it during his lifetime.[8, 9, 10] Descartes later stated that heliocentrism formed the "entire foundations" of his philosophy.[11] In his 1644 work, *Principles of Philosophy*, however, he reconciled his ideas with Church doctrine by asserting that the Earth does not move.[12] Only after his death was *Treatise on Light* published in 1664, openly affirming the heliocentric view and the Earth's motion. This episode reveals how institutional pressure shapes not only public doctrine but private thought.

While Copernicus, Galileo, and Descartes transformed astronomy and natural philosophy, Francis Bacon (1561–1626) addressed something deeper: the structure of the human mind itself. In *The Advancement of Learning* (1605) and later in *Novum Organum* (1620), Bacon argues that reliable knowledge is difficult to attain because the mind is shaped by inherited patterns of thought, along with the prejudices and collective assumptions that accompany them.

In *The Advancement of Learning,* Bacon outlines several key benefits of genuine learning. First, learning safeguards people from ignorance and error. Second, it benefits the mind just as exercise benefits the body. Third, learning is pleasurable in and of itself. Fourth, it makes the mind gentle, generous, and flexible, whereas ignorance makes it rude, decayed, and defiant. Fifth, learning applies knowledge to human conduct in ways that bring reward and comfort. Sixth, it ministers to the diseases of the mind, providing healing and remedies. Seventh, learning prevents the mind from becoming fixed or rigid, allowing it to remain open to growth and transformation. Finally, learning helps a person grow into a better and more thoughtful human being each day.[13]

In *Novum Organum,* Bacon famously declares that "knowledge is power," yet he warns that the pursuit of knowledge is often distorted by what he calls the "idols of the mind."[14, 15] He identifies four such idols—the Theater, the Marketplace, the Cave, and the Tribe—as false mental constructs that shape human thinking.[16, 17] These idols arise from authority, language, identity, and human nature.[18] They frame perception, distort reasoning, and obstruct understanding—forming systems of belief that we often accept without question.

The Scientific Revolution, therefore, was not simply a series of discoveries. It was an epistemological awakening. It revealed that entire frameworks of knowledge can appear coherent, authoritative, and complete—while remaining fundamentally flawed. The Aristotelian–Ptolemaic world functioned as an Idol of the Theater: a system sustained not because it was empirically verified, but because it had become institutionalized, normalized, and psychologically embedded.

The lesson remains relevant. Frames of knowledge do not persist solely through evidence; they endure because they shape the human mind, and the shaped mind, in turn, defends them.

This first book of Volume One, *Systems of Science*, examines the origins of life and explores how authority-imposed frameworks shape our understanding. It also asks a Baconian question: when alternative narratives are presented, are they dismissed because they are false or because they challenge authority?

This book begins on Earth (Chapters 1–3), extends into space (Chapters 4–6), and returns to Earth (Chapter 7), tracing how authority, anomaly, and interpretation interact across disciplines. Drawing on catastrophism, paleoanthropology, evolutionary biology, molecular biology, astrobiology, archaeology, geology, and space exploration—alongside alternative perspectives such as creationism and extraterrestrial disclosure—the analysis compares mainstream and dissenting narratives. The aim is to show how systems determine what may be considered legitimate knowledge.

Chapter 1, "Origins of Human Existence," surveys prevailing scientific explanations of human origins while also examining alternative frameworks, such as creationism and panspermia. The chapter invites reflection on how *origin narratives* are constructed and defended.

Chapter 2, "Origins of Modern Humans and Culture," explores early technological and symbolic developments, the Last Glacial Period, the Younger Dryas, and the Impact Hypotheses. It examines discoveries such as Göbekli Tepe, which challenge linear models of cultural progression.

Chapter 3, "Has Human Civilization Progressed?" approaches the concept of progress through alternative archaeology, astrophysics, and investigative journalism. The discussion culminates in the Kardashev Scale, which measures civilizations by energy capacity.

Chapters 4 and 5 turn to the Moon—its geological anomalies, speculative interpretations, and claims of suppressed information. These chapters examine how evidence is evaluated, classified, or dismissed.

Chapter 6, "Voyager 1," highlights a technological triumph that symbolizes both scientific ambition and existential curiosity. Its journey into interstellar space invites reflection on humanity's desire to explore, understand, and represent itself beyond Earth.

Chapter 7, "The Alien Question," considers whether myths, monuments, and modern testimonies suggest contact with extraterrestrial intelligence and its influence on human civilization.

Chapter 8, "What Does It All Mean?" concludes by urging intellectual humility. It invites readers to hold knowledge provisionally—to recognize that explanatory systems, however persuasive, remain subject to revision.

The Scientific Revolution teaches that progress does not come from rejecting authority outright, but from recognizing its limits. Bacon did not advocate abandoning systems of knowledge; he urged that they be held tentatively, always open to correction. Many contemporary debates may arise not from a lack of evidence, but from tension between emerging anomalies and entrenched explanatory structures.

This book invites readers to adopt the posture that defined the best of the Scientific Revolution: disciplined skepticism, methodological openness, and a willingness to question even the most convincing stages upon which reality appears to be set.

VOLUME ONE
Idols of the Theater
Systems Imposed by Authority

Book 1
Systems of Science

CHAPTER 1

Origins of Human Existence

Let's step back in time—not just thousands, but millions of years. Long before recorded history, cities, or even spoken language, the first clues to our origins began to emerge in the form of upright-walking ancestors who lived in Africa.

Around 3.2 million years ago, a small-bodied, bipedal hominin named "Lucy" lived in what is now Ethiopia.[19] She belonged to the species *Australopithecus afarensis*. Though not human, Lucy was a crucial ancestor—a bridge between earlier primates and the genus *Homo*, to which modern humans belong.

About 2 million years ago, *Homo habilis* had emerged, followed by *Homo erectus* around 1.8 million years ago.[20] *Homo erectus* marked a remarkable evolutionary step: it was the first hominin to control fire, build advanced tools, and migrate out of Africa into Europe. This species survived for over a million years, until around 250,000 years ago, giving rise to several later human species.[21]

Section 1: Did Humans Nearly Go Extinct?

A provocative theory published in 2023 suggests that ancient humans came alarmingly close to extinction around 900,000 years ago.[22] According to genetic evidence, our early ancestors may have dwindled to as few as 1,280 breeding individuals—a narrow escape that could have changed the course of human evolution forever.[23]

This potential crisis occurred during a dramatic shift in Earth's climate known as the Mid-Pleistocene Transition, when glacial cycles became longer and harsher.[24] Global cooling, shrinking habitats, and environmental stress may have drastically reduced food sources and livable land, pushing early humans to the brink.[25] The population decline was not a short-term disaster, but a prolonged bottleneck that lasted 117,000 years.[26] Somehow, a small group managed to survive through this period, preserving the genetic thread that would eventually lead to modern humans.[27]

These early humans were not yet *Homo sapiens*, but likely late *Homo erectus* or early *Homo heidelbergensis*—a species considered to be a common ancestor of modern humans, Neanderthals, and Denisovans.[28] The fossil record from this period is sparse, especially in Africa, which adds to the mystery. However, traits associated with *Homo heidelbergensis* begin to appear after this bottleneck, suggesting they may have emerged from this small surviving population.[29]

Section 2: Rise of Modern Humans

Homo heidelbergensis lived between roughly 600,000 and 200,000 years ago.[30] They had larger brains than their predecessors, crafted more advanced tools, and hunted cooperatively. Their descendants diverged into distinct lineages: Neanderthals (*Homo neanderthalensis*) in Europe, Denisovans (*Homo denisova*) in North Asia, and modern humans (*Homo sapiens*) in East Africa.[31, 32, 33]

Modern humans first appeared around 300,000 years ago. Fossil evidence from Jebel Irhoud, Morocco, supports this timeline.[34] For most of our history, early modern humans lived in small, mobile bands of hunter-gatherers, relying on their deep knowledge of the environment and strong social cooperation to survive.

Section 3: Crossing Continents

It wasn't until between 100,000 and 70,000 years ago that modern humans began migrating out of Africa.[35] By around 50,000 to 40,000 years ago, they had reached Asia, Europe, and Australia. Along the way, they encountered other hominins, including Neanderthals and Denisovans, and interbred with them.[36] As a result, many non-African populations today carry small percentages of Neanderthal or Denisovan DNA—genetic traces of these ancient interactions.[37, 38] Denisovans disappeared around 40,000 years ago, whereas Neanderthals became extinct around 30,000 years ago.[39]

Section 4: Cosmic Catastrophe and Extinction

In *The Cycle of Cosmic Catastrophes*, Richard Firestone proposes that a supernova exploded about 41,000 years ago roughly 200 light-years from Earth, setting off a chain of effects that later reached the planet.[40] A supernova is a powerful and luminous explosion that occurs during the final evolutionary stages of a massive star.

Firestone argues that the event would have dramatically altered the sky, as cosmic rays from the explosion illuminated the atmosphere and produced vivid colors. He suggests that a bright new star—"larger than the Moon"—appeared and grew increasingly luminous for twenty-one days as the expanding dust cloud thinned.[41] The supernova's remnant, he claims, remained visible in the night sky for about a decade.[42] According to Firestone, the resulting radiation exposure caused stress and injury in living organisms, leading to DNA damage, reduced fertility, mutations, and death.[43]

He further contends that high-energy particles from the supernova eventually reached Earth, increasing cosmic-ray intensity and cloud formation, which in turn triggered climatic change. Firestone argues that this led to a sudden drop in ocean temperatures, plunging Earth into its coldest climate in 150,000 years.[44] He links this period to major megafaunal extinctions in Australia, Southeast Asia, and possibly Africa, and to significant shifts in human evolution, including the decline of Neanderthals and the emergence of modern humans from Cro-Magnon populations.[45]

Firestone also suggests that the supernova's remnants initiated a series of catastrophic cosmic events. He argues that a debris cloud eventually interacted with the solar system, producing cosmic rays and particles that appeared as radiocarbon spikes in Earth sediments, and culminated in a comet or comet-like object striking Earth around 13,000 years ago.[46] He attributes this impact to the megafaunal extinctions and the abrupt disappearance of Paleo-Indians and Clovis peoples associated with the Younger Dryas event.[47]

While the direct lethality of radiation is clear, Firestone proposes that the supernova's broader influence occurred indirectly through mutation.[48] He claims that early humans possessed only O+ blood, which remains the most common blood type worldwide today, comprising 38–42% of the global population.[49] He suggests that mutations around the time of the supernova produced A+ and B+ blood types, now representing roughly 30% and 15% of the population, respectively, with the remaining 13–17% representing all other blood types combined (O–, A–, B–, AB+, AB–).[50]

Firestone further argues that DNA evidence indicates type O blood is widespread, especially in North, South, and Central America, while type B likely originated in Central Asia or Africa, and type A appears to have roots in Europe, Canada, and Australia.[51] Citing a 1982 study, he notes that genetic evidence suggests Asian and Caucasian populations diverged about 41,000 years ago, implying a major mutation occurred at that time.[52] The same study, he adds, claims that all Paleo-Indians descended from a small group of survivors of a severe population decline, or "bottleneck."[53]

Many geneticists agree that humanity experienced a significant population reduction between 70,000 and 30,000 years ago, commonly attributed to the eruption of the Toba supervolcano in Southeast Asia (present-day Sumatra, Indonesia) around 74,000 years ago.[54] The Toba catastrophe theory argues that the human population may have dropped from perhaps a million to fewer than "several thousand" individuals.[55]

Firestone, however, offers an alternative explanation, suggesting that radiation from the supernova could account for the bottleneck. He contends that genetic and blood-type evidence indicates a surge of mutations in Asia and Europe around 41,000 years ago.[56]

Recently, some scientists—most notably Sanja Panovska—presenting at the European Geosciences Union General Assembly have shown increased openness to Firestone's hypothesis of a supernova event around 41,000 years ago.[57] Supporting research points to a period of "magnetic field excursions," during which Earth's magnetic field weakened significantly, nearly disappearing around that time in what is known as the "Laschamps excursion."[58] This episode was marked by unusually low magnetic field intensity, suggesting reduced protection of Earth's surface from harmful cosmic radiation.[59] The diminished shielding would have led to increased production of "cosmogenic radionuclides" in the atmosphere.[60]

Section 5: Youth of Our Species

When placed in the broader context of Earth's 4.5-billion-year history, humanity's presence is strikingly recent. Consider that sharks, for example, have existed for over 400 million years—more than 100 million years longer than octopuses, over 200 million years before the appearance of dinosaurs, and nearly 1,000 times longer than modern humans. Emerging during the Devonian period, sharks have survived five mass extinctions, including the one that wiped out the dinosaurs 66 million years ago.

Though ancient sharks looked different, their basic body structure has remained largely unchanged—a sign of evolution. As ocean conservationist Ocean Ramsey once said, humanity is "just a blink in geological time" compared to life forms like sharks.[61]

We are humbled by the profound realization that human existence stretches back 300,000 years, while our individual lives—just 75 years—are but a fleeting moment, a heartbeat in the endless flow of time. Therefore, it may be beneficial to live with a sense of purpose rather than simply following prevailing trends. Even when circumstances or social norms seem to move in a particular direction, individuals can make intentional choices that reflect their own values, interests, and long-term goals, whether or not those choices align with the mainstream.

Understanding our place in this deep biological history fosters humility and curiosity. While humans have achieved incredible technological and cultural feats in a relatively short time, the planet's ancient inhabitants remind us how young we really are.

Section 6: Theories of the Origin of Human Existence

This section explores four main theories regarding the origins of human existence—abiogenesis, creationism, natural selection, and panspermia—as they have appeared throughout history, from ancient times to the present. Each advances a claim grounded in scientific investigation; however, these claims are best regarded as provisional ideas rather than final conclusions, encouraging inquiry and reflection while fostering a deeper appreciation of who we are, where we may have come from, and where we might be going.

1. *Abiogenesis: Life from Non-Life*

The question of how life began has fascinated thinkers for millennia. More than 2,600 years before Darwin, the Greek philosopher Xenophanes may have been the first to recognize the true significance of fossils. He observed what he described as "an impression of a fish and of seaweed" and noted that these forms had been left behind "when everything was long ago covered with mud, and the impression was dried in the mud."[62]

The idea that the Earth's surface was once composed of mud or slime was not new. It was a hallmark among the natural philosophers, possibly originating with Thales, who believed that all things possess a "moist nature."[63] Anaximander expanded on this view by proposing that life began in mud.[64]

Aristotle was the first to propose a theory of "spontaneous generation"—the idea that living organisms can arise from nonliving matter without parents or reproduction.[65] He observed that while many animals reproduce from parents, others appeared to emerge directly from decaying organic material under the right conditions.[66] For instance, he noted that flies originated from larvae in manure when moisture, heat, and decomposition were present.[67, 68]

Aristotle's explanation reflected a broader system of thought: natural teleology, the belief that nature acts with purpose. Life, in his view, arose not by chance, but according to principles inherent in the conditions he observed.[69] His framework interpreted natural phenomena in terms of purpose, order, and observable regularities for understanding the natural world.

The combination of these ideas—the moist nature of all things, the origin of life in mud, the discovery of fossil impressions, and the principle of spontaneous generation—demonstrates how explanatory systems shape our understanding of the origin of existence. These early speculations foreshadowed what is now called abiogenesis: the scientific theory that life arose naturally from nonliving chemical compounds on Earth roughly 3.5 billion years ago through gradual chemical evolution and increasing complexity.[70]

In the modern era, the first systematic model for abiogenesis emerged in the 1920s, when Alexander Oparin and J.B.S. Haldane, working independently, proposed a theory of "chemical evolution."[71] They suggested that life began with the formation of organic molecules in the early oceans of Earth—what later came to be known more colloquially as the prebiotic or primordial soup.[72] This molecular evolution occurred in a "liquid" medium associated with "coacervate droplets," under the continuous input of free energy from external sources such as sunlight or lightning, which sustained and drove the processes that led to life.[73] In the chapter summary of his 1924 book *The Origin of Life,* Oparin writes:

These organic substances [i.e., carbon, hydrogen, oxygen,
and nitrogen] are endowed with tremendous chemical
potentialities, and they entered a variety of chemical
reactions... As a consequence of these complex reactions,
high-molecular organic compounds were produced similar
to those which at the present time compose the organism of
animals and plants.[74]

Oparin suggests that the origin of life involves three key components: (1)
the spontaneous formation of complex organic compounds—composed of
carbon, hydrogen, oxygen, and nitrogen—that constitute living organisms;
(2) the emergence of complex chemical reactions that support biological
functions; and (3) the continuous input of free energy to sustain and drive
these processes.[75]

This theoretical framework set the stage for experimental scientific
research into abiogenesis. In 1952, Stanley Miller, under the mentorship of
Harold Urey, sought to test the Oparin-Haldane hypothesis.[76] The Miller-
Urey experiment supports the theory of chemical evolution. They designed
an experiment to simulate the conditions of the early Earth's atmosphere—
believed at the time to be reducing, composed mainly of methane (CH_4),
ammonia (NH_3), water vapor (H_2O), and hydrogen gas (H_2)—and exposed
this gaseous mixture to continuous electrical sparks, intended to simulate
lightning.[77, 78]

This specific gas mixture was chosen for several reasons: (1) CH_4, NH_3,
H_2O, and H_2 had been detected in the atmospheres of Jupiter and Saturn
since the 1930s; (2) the primitive atmospheres of these gas giants were
thought to resemble that of early Earth; and (3) because Jupiter and Saturn
are cold and distant from the Sun, it is inferred that they have retained
their original compositions.[79] Therefore, Miller and Urey concluded that
the current compositions of the atmospheres of Jupiter and Saturn serve as
reasonable proxies for Earth's primitive atmosphere.[80]

The results were groundbreaking. After a week of running the
apparatus, Miller and Urey found several amino acids, including glycine

and alanine—the basic building blocks of proteins.[81] This demonstrated, for the first time, that organic molecules could form spontaneously under prebiotic conditions. Their findings were published in *Science* in 1953, in a paper titled "A Production of Amino Acids Under Possible Primitive Earth Conditions."[82]

The Miller-Urey experiment marked a turning point in the study of life's origins. It provided the first experimental support for the theory of abiogenesis and ushered in the "first experimental program" in the field.[83] It also helped define the idea that life could arise through natural chemical processes, guided not by a blueprint or divine design, but by the physical and chemical properties of matter under the right environmental conditions.

Despite the experiment's success, abiogenesis remains an incomplete theory. While it helps explain how life's basic components—like amino acids—might have formed, it does not account for the emergence of self-replicating systems, cell membranes, or consciousness. The Miller-Urey experiment shows only one possible pathway for the formation of life's building blocks, not the full journey from chemistry to biology.[84]

Still, from a historical and scientific perspective, the Miller-Urey experiment stands as a landmark. It exemplifies the transition from speculative philosophy to empirical science in the study of life's origins, and it underscores the value of linking theoretical insights to experimental methods. Moreover, teaching this history in narrative form helps students better grasp how scientific theories evolve and why they matter.[85]

2. *Creationism: Divine Origin of Humanity*

About 2,500 years ago, the Greek philosopher Anaxagoras was among the first to introduce a rational principle, Mind, which he described as "a divine machine for making the world."[86] Aristotle recognized Anaxagoras's appeal to a rational and intelligent cause—Mind—as a fundamental principle underlying the order of the cosmos. He stated that Anaxagoras introduced the idea that Mind exists throughout nature, just as it does in animals, and is responsible for the order of the world.[87]

Historically, such ideas were not always met with curiosity. In the sixteenth century, the Italian philosopher and cosmologist Giordano Bruno proposed a thought that now seems almost self-evident: the existence of an infinite universe and innumerable worlds, a position he defended in his 1591 work *On the Infinite Universe and Worlds*.[88] His claim was not merely an astronomical conjecture but a profound challenge to the accepted beliefs and authorities of his time, for imagining other worlds—possibly inhabited and capable of hosting life—was to question Earth's uniqueness and humanity's central place in the cosmos.

Unsurprisingly, this challenge provoked a harsh response from those in power. Consequently, Bruno's conviction confronted the religious and political authorities that governed knowledge, and it was treated as a dangerous heresy. He was condemned and executed by being burned alive at the stake in the streets of Rome in 1600. Bruno's fate reminds us how revolutionary and controversial the suggestion of extraterrestrial life once was, since even entertaining the possibility of life beyond Earth was considered a profound threat to established beliefs and authority.

The conflict between science and religious authority did not end with Bruno. It was not until 1632—more than three decades later—that Galileo published *Dialogue Concerning the Two Chief World Systems*, as mentioned in the Introduction to this book. The work defended heliocentrism—the view that the Earth and other planets orbit the Sun, rather than the Sun and planets orbiting the Earth. By challenging church authority, the book directly led to Galileo's trial in 1633 and his conviction by the Roman Inquisition. He was forced to recant and spent the remainder of his life under house arrest.

In the centuries that followed, scientific knowledge continued to expand, revealing just how immense the cosmos truly is. Scientists generally agree that the universe is far older than the Earth, estimating its age at approximately 14 billion years compared with the Earth's formation around 4.5 billion years ago. This vast difference in timescales suggests that countless worlds may have existed long before our planet came into existence. Moreover, astronomers estimate that the Milky Way galaxy contains roughly 400 billion stars, and current observations indicate that most stars host at least one planet, implying the existence of potentially hundreds of billions of exoplanets within our galaxy alone.[89]

Given the vastness of cosmic time and the abundance of planets, it is plausible that life—and possibly intelligence—arose elsewhere long before humanity appeared. From this perspective, it is reasonable to ask whether life may have originated elsewhere prior to the emergence of humans.

This scientific understanding has significant implications for how we view creation. Creationism is a theory that offers a theological explanation for human origins, grounded in the belief that a divine being—commonly identified as God—intentionally created humanity. In the Judeo-Christian tradition, the Book of Genesis describes God forming man and woman in His own image—a concept known as *Imago Dei*.[90] This concept is not grounded in what some might suggest, such as moral awareness, a spiritual soul, or anthropomorphic traits, but rather in intellect and will, which reflect the Creator's intellectual nature.[91, 92]

However, within creationist thought, there is not a single unified interpretation. There are three primary forms of creationism: Young Earth Creationism (YEC), Old Earth Creationism (OEC), and Intelligent Design Creationism (IDC). YEC adherents interpret the biblical timeline literally, holding that the Earth is between 6,000 and 10,000 years old as described in the Genesis narrative, though geocentrism—while argued by some biblical literalists—is not a defining belief of contemporary YEC.[93]

OEC offers a middle ground, accepting some scientific evidence while maintaining divine intervention. OEC supporters accept the scientific evidence for an ancient Earth—billions of years old—while maintaining that God is a "direct causal agent of observed changes."[94] Even though OEC's accept most of modern physics, chemistry, and geology, they are not very dissimilar to YEC's in their rejection of biological evolution.[95]

IDC takes a different approach by focusing on the complexity of life. IDC proponents argue that life is too complex to have evolved "by chance" and often point to the complex, information-rich structure of DNA as evidence of an intelligent designer.[96] IDC advocates assert that information cannot spontaneously arise from matter or random chance; rather, it must originate from intelligence. Intricate design, they argue, cannot occur through unguided natural processes.[97]

To understand why creationism remains persuasive to many, we must look at how the universe appears to us. Look up at the sky and reflect on all that surrounds you. Creationists also point to the Earth's placement in the cosmos as further evidence of intentional design. When we consider the position of our planet in relation to the sun and the other planets in our solar system, the contrast is striking. Earth alone, with its delicate balance of conditions, supports life. Its temperature, atmosphere, magnetic field, and distance from the sun create a perfect environment for living organisms to thrive.

When we compare Earth to its neighboring planets, the contrast becomes even clearer. Venus, similar in size to Earth, is shrouded in thick clouds of sulfuric acid and has a surface temperature hot enough to melt lead—around 900°F (475°C). Its crushing atmospheric pressure makes life impossible. Mars, often called Earth-like, is a frozen desert with a thin, carbon dioxide-filled atmosphere. It lacks surface water, magnetic protection, and conditions necessary for sustaining life without advanced technology.

The outer planets are even more inhospitable. Jupiter, a massive ball of hydrogen and helium, has no solid surface and deadly radiation belts. Saturn, with its iconic rings, is equally inhospitable—cold, stormy, and without a surface.

Even the most distant planets in our system show how unique Earth is. Uranus and Neptune, the outermost planets, are frozen gas giants. Uranus's extreme tilt causes radical seasonal changes, while Neptune is a turbulent, icy world with violent storms. Both are far too cold and toxic to support any form of life.

In contrast, Earth is remarkably comfortable and stable, with an average temperature of 60°F. The hottest recorded temperature is 130°F in

Death Valley, while the coldest reaches -128.6°F in Antarctica. Earth has a breathable atmosphere, an abundance of liquid water, a balanced climate, and protective systems—from the ozone layer to the magnetosphere—that shield life from the dangers of space. It's Moon helps stabilize the planet's tilt, moderating the seasons, while its distance from the sun allows just the right amount of energy to reach the surface—not too much, not too little.

From a creationist perspective, this balance is evidence of deliberate design. The other planets highlight what Earth is not—and in doing so, they emphasize just how unique, fine-tuned, and hospitable our planet is. In their view, this remarkable alignment of conditions supports the idea that Earth was created with purpose—for life, and ultimately, for humanity.

Yet many scientists challenge these claims as lacking empirical support. Creationism is often grounded in religious texts, particularly the Bible, and is viewed by many scientists as a belief system rather than a scientific theory. Key claims—such as a young Earth or the sudden appearance of fully formed species—conflict with substantial evidence from geology, genetics, and the fossil record. Transitional fossils, radiometric dating, and shared genetic markers all support evolution and point to an ancient Earth, far older than a literal interpretation of Genesis would suggest.

Critics also argue that creationist arguments ignore broader cosmic context. Creationists often highlight Earth's precise conditions for life—its ideal distance from the sun, protective atmosphere, and stable environment—as evidence of divine design. However, this view overlooks natural explanations, including the anthropic principle, which states that we observe Earth's suitability for life simply because we are here to observe it. From the critics' perspective, pointing to Earth's uniqueness without considering billions of other uninhabitable planets in the universe can lead to biased conclusions.

Moreover, the diversity of life on Earth shows that life can adapt to unexpected conditions. It is a misconception to assume that life can only exist in conditions similar to those on Earth—namely, with water and oxygen.[98] Some life forms on Earth, such as anaerobic bacteria, survive without oxygen.[99] Others have adapted to live in extreme environments, including the toxic water near nuclear reactors.[100]

If we broaden our perspective by reversing it, we may realize that our view and understanding of "habitability" is limited. Beings from another planet might view *their* own extreme conditions—such as temperatures of -150 to -200°C—as necessary for life. They might find Earth's environment just as hostile as we would theirs.[101]

Scientific experiments further support the idea that life can exist under extreme conditions. In the 1950s, entomologists Hinton and Blum exposed a species of midge to extreme environments, including high levels of radiation and temperatures. They dehydrated the insects at 100°C, then immersed them in liquid helium—a substance as cold as outer space. Even after heavy radiation exposure, the midges resumed normal life functions and reproduced healthy offspring.[102]

Similarly, laboratory simulations show life can thrive in environments unlike those on Earth. In the 1970s, biologist Sanford Siegel simulated Jupiter's atmosphere in a laboratory—an environment rich in ammonia, methane, and hydrogen. Remarkably, he was able to breed bacteria and mites in these conditions, and the substances did not harm the organisms.[103]

These scientific insights raise a profound theological question. Creationism asserts that God created the Earth, the universe, the planets, the galaxies—everything that exists. But if God is the architect of all things, then what makes humanity so special? Why would an all-powerful being, responsible for the vastness of space and time—400 billion stars in our Milky Way and potentially billions of habitable planets, plus two trillion galaxies in the observable universe—take a personal interest in us?

This idea—that humanity is uniquely significant in the grand scheme—echoes the ancient belief of Earth as the literal geocentric center of the universe. While scientific discovery eventually dismantled that view, many who hold to a creationist perspective continue to retain its emotional core. They maintain that humanity occupies a central, privileged place in creation. Even though Earth is an ordinary planet, orbiting an average-sized star 30,000 light-years from the center of the Milky Way, this perspective remains convinced that our planet is the center of it all.

It's as if we hold a claim, entitlement, or monopoly on divine attention—despite the immensity of the cosmos suggesting otherwise. The persistence of this belief raises a critical question. Why would the creator of a billion galaxies care so intimately about one species on one small planet?

So, what does this say about our sense of spiritual importance? Is our sense of spiritual centrality rooted in truth, or is it another echo of our ancient, geocentric pride—repackaged in theological terms?

Finally, critics argue that creationism may hinder scientific progress by attributing natural phenomena to divine design, thereby replacing scientific inquiry with faith-based answers.

Yet creationism remains meaningful to many people. It continues to resonate with many who see it as offering moral guidance, purpose, and a deeper sense of meaning—answers that science, for all its explanatory power, may not fully address.

3. *Darwinian Evolution: Theory of Natural Selection*

The question of how human beings have evolved over time has intrigued scientists for centuries. Among the many proposed explanations, Darwinian evolution through natural selection—often referred to as the theory of "evolutionary biology"—remains the most scientifically strong and widely accepted model for explaining the origin and development of human life.[104]

Charles Darwin was a scientist who began a pivotal journey at the age of 22. From 1831 to 1836, he sailed on a five-year expedition aboard the HMS Beagle, traveling to South America, Australia, and Africa. During this voyage, he observed a vast array of life forms in their natural habitats, carefully studying their diversity.[105]

After more than two decades of research and evidence gathering, Darwin published *On the Origin of Species by Means of Natural Selection or*

The Preservation of Favoured Races in the Struggle for Life in 1859, introducing his groundbreaking theory of evolution.

Darwin observed that no two individuals within a species are exactly alike. While they share a common form, each exhibits variations in traits.[106] He recognized a constant interaction between organisms and their environment, noting that not all individuals born will survive, as they must compete for limited resources. Those with traits better suited to their environment are more likely to survive and reproduce—this is known as being "fit" for their environment.[107]

Darwin recognized that variation does not arise from an individual's ability to change during its lifetime, but instead exists naturally among individuals in a population and is passed down to offspring.[108] He observed that within every species, there is a natural and *"diversified variability"*—differences such as size, strength, speed, and coloration.[109, 110] These variations are both "favorable" and "profitable" because they are often heritable by the surviving offspring of an organism.[111] According to Darwin, "if any one species does not become modified and improved in a corresponding degree with its competitors, it will soon be exterminated."[112]

He called this process "natural selection"—the means by which species evolve over time—as individuals with favorable trait variations are more likely to survive and reproduce.[113, 114, 115] Over many generations, these favorable traits become more common, leading to the gradual adaptation of species to their environments. Darwin referred to this long-term process as "descent with modification through natural selection," a concept central to the mainstream understanding of evolution.[116]

Darwin's concept of "descent with modification" explains how species evolve over time through accumulated adaptations to the environment. He implies this idea in several places throughout *On the Origin of Species*. In his Introduction, Darwin explains that because more individuals are born than can survive, there is a "recurring struggle for existence." As a result, any organism that varies in even a slight but beneficial way has a better chance of surviving and being *"naturally selected"*[117]

Darwin reinforces this idea in Chapter 1, where he emphasizes the "accumulative" nature of selection. He notes that nature produces "successive variations," while selection acts by adding them up in directions that are "useful."[118] This shows how small changes, preserved over time, can lead to significant differences.

In Chapter 14, Darwin further stresses that natural selection works only by "accumulating slight, successive, favorable variations" and cannot produce sudden or dramatic modification; it can act only by "very short and slow steps."[119] Later in the same chapter, he extends this principle to all life, stating that all organic beings that have ever lived "descended from a single primordial form."[120]

Together, these passages illustrate Darwin's argument that species arise through descent with modification by the gradual accumulation of adaptations to the environment through natural selection.

The concept "descent with modification," also emphasizes that all species share a common ancestry and suggests that humans, like all other species, are the result of possibly millions of years of gradual change from earlier life forms. Darwin does not state this directly, but he strongly implies it in a brief paragraph near the end of the final chapter in *On the Origin of Species*. He writes:

> In the distant future, I see open fields for far more important researches. Psychology will be based on a new foundation, that of the necessary acquirement of each mental power and capacity by gradation. Light will be thrown on the origin of man and his history.[121]

Throughout most of the book, Darwin avoids explicitly discussing human evolution, likely due to the controversial nature of the topic at the time. However, in Chapter 7, he addresses the concepts of "descent" and "gradations"—principles that clearly apply to all organisms, including humans.[122]

Following the publication of *On the Origin of Species*, many misconceptions about natural selection and evolution emerged—some of which still persist to this day. A common misunderstanding is the belief that humans descended directly from monkeys.[123] Humans and monkeys share a common ancestor but evolved along different paths.

Another widespread misconception is the idea that the structure and order of nature are divinely preordained, rather than the result of environmental change and adaptation.[124] The debate over evolution is not about whether change occurs over time, but rather *how* it occurs.[125]

Additionally, Darwin's contemporaries often misinterpreted natural selection as a goal-directed process.[126] Some extended his ideas into human society, giving rise to what became known as "Social Darwinism."[127] This distorted interpretation claimed that social success was evidence of biological superiority, promoting the notion that society functioned on the principle of "survival of the fittest."[128] This was a major misrepresentation of Darwin's theory.

In truth, evolution by natural selection is neutral and not goal-oriented.[129] It does not strive for improvement or create "higher" or "lower" forms of life.[130] All living organisms have equally evolved in the sense that they have each adapted to their specific environments over time. Evolution does not plan for the future and should not be confused with progress.[131] Darwin emphasized that "descent with modification through natural selection" leads to better adaptation of organisms to their specific environments—not to any abstract notion of advancement, such as increasing complexity or diversity.[132]

Darwin's theory places humanity within the broader context of the natural world, emphasizing our deep connection to all living things. He himself held a profound reverence for nature, as reflected in his words:

> There is a grandeur in this view of life, with its several
> powers, having been originally breathed into a few forms or
> into one; and that, whilst this planet has gone cycling on
> according to the fixed law of gravity, from so simple a

beginning endless forms most beautiful and most wonderful
have been, and are being evolved.[133]

Darwin suggests that life's richness is not opposed to order, but generated by it. The same unchanging laws that govern the cosmos also carry within them the capacity for endless becoming.

Darwinian evolution does not directly address the origin of life or the first appearance of humans. It begins with the assumption that life already exists. Yet, as new discoveries in genetics, paleontology, and anthropology continue to emerge, Darwin's ideas remain central to our understanding of how we have evolved.

4. *Panspermia—Extraterrestrial Intervention*

Prometheus, the fifth film in the *Alien* franchise but chronologically first, opens with a symbolic act of creation. On a young, uninhabitable Earth, an alien ingests a black liquid, disintegrates, and seeds life with his DNA— implying that an advanced species may have engineered humanity.[134]

Fast forward to 2089, when archaeologists Dr. Elizabeth Shaw and Dr. Charlie Holloway discover 35,000-year-old paintings in Scotland, depicting star maps also found in other ancient cultures. Shaw believes these are invitations from humanity's creators.[135]

By 2093, the spaceship Prometheus arrives at the moon LV-223, located in the Zeta 2 Reticuli star system 34.6 light-years from Earth, after a two-year journey at nearly the speed of light.[136] The crew seeks out the Engineers, an alien race believed to have created humanity not through evolution, but through genetic manipulation.

In real-world science, modern humans appeared around 300,000 to 200,000 years ago in Africa, marking the beginning of our species' existence.[137] After the extinction of the Neanderthals around 30,000 years ago, modern humans rapidly advanced.[138] Around 30,000 years ago, a sudden cultural and technological leap began, culminating in the construction of Göbekli Tepe around 11,600 years ago (9600 BCE), and eventually space exploration.[139]

This sudden acceleration raises a fundamental question: Was it the result of natural evolution—or some form of intervention? Perhaps it was both.

First proposed by the Greek philosopher Anaxagoras 2,500 years ago, the theory of panspermia holds that the "seeds" (spermata) of all things, including life, exist throughout the cosmos. This suggests a form of panspermia, though not in the modern biological sense.[140] Only much later was this idea reinterpreted to suggest that life originated elsewhere in the universe and reached Earth via comets or meteorites carrying microbial material.[141, 142]

Derived from the Greek words *pan* (all) and *sperma* (seed), the term *panspermia* denotes the view that the universe is permeated with life-bearing principles dispersed across celestial bodies such as comets, meteors, and interstellar dust. This opens the door to the possibility that we share a cosmic ancestry.

One of the earliest modern proponents of panspermia was Swedish chemist Svante Arrhenius, who won the Nobel Prize in 1908. At the time, the prevailing theory of life's origin was abiogenesis. Arrhenius, however, proposed that microscopic life could survive the harsh conditions of space and travel across the cosmos, potentially seeding life on planets like ours.[143]

Zircon crystals, some dating back 4.4 billion years, offer a glimpse into Earth's earliest conditions.[144] Remarkably, a 4.1-billion-year-old zircon was found to contain carbon signatures consistent with biological activity—suggesting life may have existed during the Hadean Eon, a time when Earth endured frequent impacts from space debris.[145] According to panspermia, these very impacts may have delivered the building blocks of life to our planet.

The evolving understanding of comets has played a central role in this theory. Once thought to be inert "dirty snowballs," comets are now known to contain organic molecules.[146] English astronomer Sir Fred Hoyle, renowned for his work on stellar nucleosynthesis, was also a leading proponent of panspermia. He argued that not only are we "made of stardust," but that comets may serve as incubators for life, carrying microorganisms across the galaxy.[147]

Evidence supporting Hoyle's claims emerged in 1986 when the European Space Agency's Giotto mission analyzed Halley's Comet.[148] Alongside expected gases like water vapor and methane, the probe detected hydrogen cyanide—a precursor to amino acids—and mysterious CHON particles (composed of carbon, hydrogen, oxygen, and nitrogen), the essential elements of organic chemistry.[149] Subsequent missions revealed even more complex molecules, including ethanol, formaldehyde, and glycine, a key amino acid found on Comet 67P by the Rosetta probe in 2004.[150] These discoveries suggest that the raw ingredients for life are common throughout our solar system.

While this process—called "accidental panspermia"—refers to the natural spread of life through space, a more controversial idea is "directed panspermia."[151] This theory posits that life was intentionally seeded on Earth by an advanced extraterrestrial civilization. The key to panspermia is DNA, for without DNA, there would be no life.[152]

Francis Crick, the 1962 Nobel Prize–winning geneticist and co-discoverer of the DNA double helix, supported the theory of directed panspermia.[153] In 1971, he attended a conference on communication with extraterrestrial intelligence hosted by Carl Sagan.[154] Along with his colleague Leslie Orgel, Crick argued that life was deliberately transmitted to Earth by intelligent beings.

In 1973, Crick and Orgel published a scientific paper titled "Directed Panspermia."[155] They argued that the chemical composition of life on Earth does not entirely match Earth's own composition. For example, they observed that certain elements essential to biology—such as the trace element molybdenum—are scarce on Earth yet abundant in meteorites.[156] This discrepancy supports the idea that life may have been engineered and introduced to Earth, suggesting that our planet may not be humanity's original home.[157] Crick further argued that the "genetic code" necessary for life may have arrived via the tail of one or more meteors or comets, implying an extraterrestrial origin for life.[158]

If this is the case, it raises questions about human evolution—particularly whether our DNA has been manipulated over thousands of years by extraterrestrials—given the emergence of modern humans in the archaeological record, from *Homo heidelbergensis* (around 600,000 years ago) to Neanderthals (400,000 years ago) to *Homo sapiens* (300,000 years ago).[159]

Mainstream archaeology acknowledges that *Homo sapiens* have existed for at least 200,000 years, yet the emergence of civilization is a relatively recent phenomenon.[160] Ancient cultures appear to have transitioned from rudimentary lifestyles to highly advanced societies in a remarkably short period of time.

Scholarly consensus, for example, suggests that the Sumerians emerged in Mesopotamia between 4500 and 4000 BCE. Within just a few centuries, they developed cities, writing, mathematics, and astronomy—achievements that, according to mainstream archaeology, predate both the Egyptian pyramids and Stonehenge by more than a thousand years. This sudden and unprecedented cultural emergence prompts a lingering question: Why didn't such a leap occur tens—or even hundreds—of thousands of years earlier? Where did this advanced knowledge come from?

Ancient texts from Sumer, Egypt, India, the Americas, and even the Bible often describe beings from the sky—gods or creators—who shaped or intervened in human development.[161] When seen through the lens of directed panspermia, these accounts take on new significance, potentially reflecting early humanity's interpretation of advanced visitors or events far beyond their understanding.

Given the growing body of evidence—from organic molecules on comets to ancient narratives of sky-beings—the idea that life on Earth originated elsewhere is no longer confined to science fiction. Whether through cosmic accident or intelligent design, panspermia offers a compelling framework for reconsidering our origins. Earth, in this view, may not be the birthplace of life, but rather one of many planets to receive its seeds.

The next time you ponder whether extraterrestrials walk among us, consider this: they may already exist within every cell of your body. If panspermia is true, then in a very real sense, *we* are the aliens.

Religious texts offer clues. Take, for example, Genesis 1:26: "Then God said, 'Let Us make man in Our image, according to Our likeness.'" Why the use of "Us" and "Our" instead of "Me" and "My"?

Who are the "giants" mentioned in Genesis 6:4—"There were giants on the earth in those days"—and who were the "sons of God" who took human women and fathered children with them?

Then in Genesis 1:31, we are told: "God saw everything that He had made, and indeed, it was very good." Yet just a few chapters later, in Genesis 6:6–22, the same Creator regrets making humanity and decides to destroy life with a great flood—sparing only Noah, his family, and the seeds of every animal. This raises a profound question: How can a Creator declare His creation "very good," then feel "sorry," and eventually decide to destroy humanity, animals, and every living creature He made? Does this suggest a non-omniscient being, one who selectively favors certain individuals, or one who simply changes His mind because He *feels* differently about His creation?

Most scholars agree that the biblical flood narrative was adapted by Moses from earlier sources—most notably, the *Epic of Gilgamesh*—and utilized it for his own ends. Moses, who likely grew up in Egypt, would have been aware of ancient Near Eastern stories resembling the creation and flood accounts. According to tradition, Moses wrote Genesis sometime between 1400 and 1200 BCE, corresponding to either a 15th-century or 13th-century Exodus, depending on how biblical texts are interpreted and how the date of the Exodus is determined.[162]

The *Epic of Gilgamesh*, however, predates Genesis by approximately 700 to 900 years, with its earliest versions dating to around 2100 BCE or about 4,000 years ago. Therefore, it is the Sumerian flood story—not the biblical one—that represents the original account.[163]

The *Epic of Gilgamesh* is one of the oldest surviving stories in the world, predating the Homeric epics by about 1,500 years. Gilgamesh himself was likely a real historical figure—a king who ruled the city of Uruk in ancient Mesopotamia around 2700 BCE.

The story follows Gilgamesh, a powerful king created by the gods as two-thirds god and one-third human.[164] After ruling as a tyrant, Gilgamesh is confronted by the gods, who create Enkidu—part beast and part man—to become his companion.[165] Together, they embark on heroic quests, defeating monsters like Humbaba and the Bull of Heaven.[166]

But when the "Anunnaki"—gods who serve as judges of fate and death—take Enkidu's life, Gilgamesh is devastated.[167] He embarks on a quest for immortality and seeks out Utnapishtim, a man granted eternal life after surviving a great flood sent by the gods.[168] Though Gilgamesh eventually fails to gain immortality, he returns home wiser, realizing that true legacy lies in one's actions and the mark left on the world.[169] A single idea runs through the story: The fear of death disturbs me.[170] The epic explores timeless themes of friendship, loss, mortality, and the search for meaning.

One compelling question that continues to puzzle scientists is why we find no concrete records of advanced civilizations prior to the end of the last Ice Age, which ended about 9600 BCE. Could there have been societies with technological capabilities that were wiped out by global cataclysms and left few traces behind?

One candidate is the Younger Dryas, a sudden global cooling event that began around 12,800 years ago and marked the end of the last 100,000-year-long Ice Age. Some alternative interpretations suggest that this event was triggered by a comet, asteroid, or meteorite explosion, leading to dramatic environmental changes and widespread ice melt.[171]

The result was rising seas, global climate disruption, mass extinctions, and widespread environmental chaos. This period aligns with flood legends found in several cultures—including Mesopotamian, Hebrew, Greek, Indian, Native American, Andean, Chinese, and Polynesian—stories that often describe divine warnings, catastrophic floods, and survival by a few.

Such stories may reflect real post-Ice Age events rather than supernatural punishment. This challenges traditional religious interpretations of the Flood and suggests a natural origin of the myth.[172]

Throughout history, whether through myth, metaphor, or scientific exploration, humanity has been driven to understand its origins. Stories of gods descending from the sky, civilizations wiped out by flood, and life seeded from the stars all reflect a deep-rooted curiosity about where we come from and what forces shaped our existence.

These narratives resonate a timeless question: Are we here by *chance,* the product of *evolution,* guided by *cosmic design,* influenced by *extraterrestrial intervention*—or shaped by a convergence of forces beyond our full understanding?

Each of these theories reflects a different way of interpreting humanity's place in the universe—whether through empirical science, spiritual belief, evolutionary biology, or speculative myth. What they all share is a deep curiosity about where we come from and why we exist. As science advances and our understanding deepens, perhaps the most important takeaway is not which theory is "right," but how our ongoing search for answers continues to shape who we are.

CHAPTER 2
Origins of Modern Humans and Culture

Neanderthals evolved approximately 400,000 years ago, while modern humans appeared around 300,000 years ago.[173] The two species coexisted between about 50,000 and 30,000 years ago, during which time they interacted, interbred, and competed.[174, 175] However, Neanderthals abruptly disappeared around 30,000 years ago.

Following this period, between roughly 70,000 and 12,000 years ago—prior to the Flood and at the dawn of the Agricultural Revolution—modern humans began forming cultures through a revolutionary development: complex language. This breakthrough, often referred to as the Cognitive Revolution, marked a pivotal moment in human history.[176]

Modern humans are inherently social animals.[177] Language enabled them not only to coordinate activities or exchange facts but, more importantly, to gossip. People talked about who liked whom, who was sleeping with whom, who could be trusted, and who was dishonest.[178] These conversations weren't trivial—they were crucial. The ability to gossip for hours helped build trust, reinforce social norms, and strengthen community bonds.[179]

Even today, much of our communication—whether via emails, phone calls, or social media—centers around gossip, often focused on alleged misconduct. Long before journalism existed, gossip acted as an early form of social accountability. In marketplaces, taverns, and communal gatherings, word of mouth identified cheaters, freeloaders, and troublemakers—functioning as the group's informal "watchdogs."[180]

What truly sets human language apart, however, is its ability to convey information about things that do not physically exist—such as legends, myths, and gods. A member of a prehistoric tribe might have said, "The lion is the guardian spirit of our tribe," just as someone today might say, "The nation must defend our freedom," or "The market will correct itself."[181] These are not tangible facts but shared beliefs—imagined realities that influence behavior and shape entire societies, reinforcing a collective perception of reality.

Cultural and technological progress evolved gradually. Over tens of thousands of years, early humans refined tools, mastered fire, practiced ritual burials, and created symbolic art. Notable examples include the *Blombos* Cave in South Africa, where engraved ochre pieces and shell beads have been found, dating back 100,000 years; the *Altamira* Cave in Spain, famous for its depictions of bison, horses, and deer, dating back 36,000 years; and the *Lascaux* Cave paintings in France, dating back 20,000 years.[182]

Section 1: Human Life in the Ice Age

Throughout this time, humans lived during the Last Glacial Period (LGP)—a prolonged phase of global cooling that lasted from about 115,000 to 11,600 years ago. The LGP was driven by Earth's long-term orbital and axial variations, known as Milankovitch cycles, which have repeated approximately every 100,000 years over the past million years.[183] These cycles triggered dramatic climatic changes, especially across the Northern Hemisphere. Regions such as North America, Europe, and Asia experienced extensive glaciation, while areas like Africa, South America, and Australia became cooler and drier.

Human societies during the LGP were primarily nomadic or semi-nomadic, relying on hunting wild animals and gathering uncultivated plants, rather than farming or domesticating animals for food. Permanent settlements had not yet formed, and survival depended on mobility and adaptation to shifting environmental conditions.

Section 2: Clovis People and the Younger Dryas

Between approximately 13,100 and 12,700 years ago, the Clovis people emerged in North America, distinguished by its advanced stone tools and technological innovation among Ice Age hunter-gatherers.[184] This culture arose shortly before the onset of the Younger Dryas—a sudden and dramatic return to glacial conditions that lasted from about 12,800 to 11,600 years ago. However, the Clovis people disappeared just as the Younger Dryas began.[185] The close timing of the Clovis rise and fall with the onset of this abrupt climate event suggests a possible link between environmental change and cultural disruption.[186]

Section 3: Great Ice Sheets of the Last Glacial Period

During the LGP, vast ice sheets dominated the Northern Hemisphere, transforming the continents of North America and Eurasia. These immense glaciers sculpted the land, altered weather patterns, and stored enormous volumes of water—water that would later flood into the oceans and reshape coastlines worldwide.

In North America, two major ice sheets prevailed: the Laurentide and the Cordilleran.[187] The Laurentide Ice Sheet was the largest, covering around 1.93 million square miles—nearly all of present-day Canada and extending deep into the northern United States. Its southern edge reached New York, Pennsylvania, Ohio, Illinois, and parts of the Missouri River Valley. It stretched eastward to the Atlantic Ocean, northward into the Arctic, and westward to the Rocky Mountains—where it met the Cordilleran Ice Sheet.

The Cordilleran Ice Sheet, while smaller, was still massive. It covered around 965,000 square miles (half the size of the Laurentide Ice Sheet). It spanned most of British Columbia, parts of the Yukon and Alaska, and extended into northern Washington, Idaho, and Montana. Unlike the broad, continuous Laurentide, the Cordilleran was shaped by mountainous terrain, giving it a more irregular, fragmented structure. Its width ranged from 300 to 620 miles, compared to the Laurentide's 2,000 miles.

In terms of thickness, the Laurentide rose about 2 to 2.5 miles from base to summit. The Cordilleran reached similar but slightly lesser heights, 1.2 to 1.9 miles.

Across the Atlantic, Europe and the Eurasian Arctic were blanketed by the Fennoscandian and Barents-Kara Ice Sheets. These two were interconnected, forming a massive glacial complex that stretched across Scandinavia and Siberia, extending into northern Germany and northwest Russia. Together, they were about half the size of the Laurentide but still reached comparable thicknesses—1.2 to 1.9 miles, similar to the Cordilleran. Their eventual melting contributed significantly to rising global sea levels, alongside the North American ice sheets.

Section 4: Glacial Lakes Missoula and Agassiz

As these ice sheets began to retreat, meltwater pooled along their southern margins, forming enormous glacial lakes. In North America, two of the most dramatic were Glacial Lake Missoula in the west and Glacial Lake Agassiz in the east.[188]

Glacial Lake Missoula stood over 4,000 feet above sea level, reached depths of at least 2,000 feet, and covered approximately 3,000 square miles.[189] Lake Missoula was formed by an ice dam in the Clark Fork Valley. Over several thousand years, between 15,000 and 12,000 years ago, the dam broke repeatedly, releasing floodwaters. However, the volume of water released during those earlier floods was tiny—like a drop in the bucket—compared to the massive final flood event 400 years later by the "Clovis comet."[190]

Glacial Lake Agassiz was larger, covering up to 170,000 square miles— bigger than any lake that exists today. However, compared to Lake Missoula, it sat at a lower elevation, between 750 and 920 feet above sea level, and was shallower, ranging from 650 to 1,000 feet deep, as it spread across a broad, shallow, and relatively flat landscape.[191]

These lakes were dammed by ice, and when those dams eventually failed, they unleashed catastrophic floods. Lake Missoula's waters roared westward toward the Pacific Ocean, while Lake Agassiz spilled eastward into the Atlantic.

Section 5: Missoula and Agassiz Floods

Living in the Pacific Northwest, I'm especially interested in the Missoula Floods. Glacial Lake Missoula, held back by a fragile ice dam, periodically burst through—an event that occurred approximately 80 times between 15,000 and 12,000 years ago, roughly once every 31 years.[192] Each flood sent torrents of water, up to 800 feet deep, crashing through narrow mountain passes and across what is now eastern Washington, reshaping the landscape.[193, 194]

These floods carved out the Channeled Scablands, widened and deepened the Columbia River Gorge, and scoured the land down to bedrock.[195] They carried with them thousands of icebergs the size of oil tankers, many embedded with house-sized boulders.[196] As the raging water swept away everything in its path—soil, vegetation, animals, and people— it permanently transformed the geography of the Pacific Northwest before finally draining into the Pacific Ocean.[197]

In the eastern region, over eighty massive glacial potholes—some reaching up to 10 feet wide and 60 feet deep—can be found along the St. Croix River in Minnesota. These features were sculpted by colossal floodwaters unleashed from the superior lobe of the Laurentide Ice Sheet. Enormous volumes of icy meltwater poured into the North Atlantic, originating from various glacial lakes. Some of this meltwater surged through the Minnesota St. Croix River, while other flows coursed directly off the Laurentide Ice Sheet into the Finger Lakes region of New York.[198]

Section 6: Understanding the Younger Dryas

Between 18,000 and 14,500 years ago, global temperatures were gradually rising, and the vast ice sheets of the LGP were steadily melting. But around 12,800 years ago, this warming trend abruptly reversed.[199] The climate suddenly plunged back into a deep freeze—particularly in the Northern Hemisphere—bringing temperatures as cold as those at the peak of the LGP. Ecosystems were dramatically reshaped, and the transition into the warmer Holocene epoch was abruptly delayed.

This intense and mysterious cold spell, known as the Younger Dryas, lasted for about 1,200 years.[200] Then, around 11,600 years ago, the climate shifted once more: global temperatures surged, the remaining ice sheets rapidly melted and collapsed into the oceans, and Earth entered a period of warmth comparable to today's.[201] The Younger Dryas marked the final phase of the LGP—a sudden, sharp interruption in the planet's otherwise steady post-Ice Age warming.

The mainstream scientific explanation attributes the Younger Dryas to disruptions in ocean circulation, likely caused by glacial meltwater entering the North Atlantic and resulting in rapid cooling.[202]

Section 7: Younger Dryas Impact Hypothesis

In contrast to the mainstream explanation, the Younger Dryas Impact Hypothesis, proposes that a comet, asteroid, or meteorite struck or exploded over North America around 12,800 years ago (as previously mentioned). According to this theory, the event triggered massive wildfires, abrupt atmospheric changes, and rapid ice melt. The resulting influx of freshwater into the oceans may have disrupted key ocean currents, initiating the Younger Dryas cooling period and causing catastrophic flooding in various parts of the world.

The hypothesis is based on alleged impact proxies—such as nanodiamonds, magnetic spherules, elevated levels of platinum, soot layers, and carbon-rich black mats—found at sites across North America and beyond, suggesting that a global event took place.[203] It doesn't directly claim that a comet melted the ice initially. Instead, the hypothesis suggests that a cooling phase came first, followed by rapid warming and the collapse of ice sheets 1,200 years later, resulting in catastrophic flooding preserved in global flood narratives, including the *Epic of Gilgamesh*, the Book of Genesis, and Plato's account of Atlantis.[204]

The Missoula and Agassiz Floods are significant to this hypothesis because they provide a compelling point of comparison for understanding large-scale, rapid environmental change associated with catastrophic events. The immense heat generated by such an impact could, in theory, trigger a dramatic destabilization of the North American ice cap.[205] Although these floods are not direct evidence of the hypothesis, their scale and timing offer important context for evaluating the plausibility of sudden disruptions to Earth's climate and landscapes.

The hypothesis further proposes that around 12,800 years ago, a high-energy event—possibly the atmospheric explosion of a comet or asteroid—may have contributed to widespread flooding and accelerated glacial melting across multiple regions. Notably, the last of the Missoula Floods occurred within this same general timeframe, near the onset of the Younger Dryas.

While the Missoula Floods are not direct evidence of an extraterrestrial impact, the fact that they unfolded so rapidly and with such force illustrates how Earth's systems are capable of undergoing large-scale changes in short periods of time. The sudden and intense nature of the Missoula Floods makes it plausible that high-energy impacts could trigger similarly rapid disruptions.

Section 8: Real-World Global Flood

Regardless of the exact cause, the melting and draining of glacial lakes worldwide around the time of the Younger Dryas 12,800 years ago contributed to a genuine global flood by releasing immense volumes of water into the oceans. This influx caused global sea levels to rise by 2 to 4 meters—not over centuries, but within just a few decades, possibly even less.[206]

To grasp the magnitude of this rise, consider that a one-meter increase in sea level today would flood major coastal cities and displace hundreds of millions of people. A four-meter rise would be catastrophic—submerging large parts of Florida, Bangladesh, the Netherlands, and flooding low-lying areas of cities like New York, London, Shanghai, and Tokyo.

This wasn't just a regional disaster—it was a planet-wide event, a true natural "world flood" caused by the collapse of massive ice sheets and the sudden release of their stored water.

Section 9: Planetary Defense—A Neglected Priority

The threat of Earth being struck by a comet—or even fragments of a comet, asteroid, or meteor—is a real and frightening possibility. A notable example is Comet Shoemaker-Levy 9, which broke apart into 21 fragments and collided with Jupiter over six days in July 1994. The impacts produced massive, fiery explosions and left dark scars on the gas giant's surface— some larger than Earth itself—that remained visible for several months.[207]

This danger is not just confined to scientific discussions. Popular films like *Armageddon* (1998) and *Don't Look Up* (2021) explore similar scenarios. In *Armageddon*, a giant asteroid threatens to destroy Earth, prompting NASA to send a team of deep-core drillers, led by Bruce Willis's character, to land on the asteroid and detonate a nuclear bomb to alter its path. In *Don't Look Up*, two scientists, played by Leonardo DiCaprio and Jennifer Lawrence, discover a comet on a collision course with Earth—an "extinction-level event" capable of wiping out humanity. Despite their warnings, they face public apathy, media distractions, and political spin, highlighting how difficult it can be to get society to take such threats seriously.

But this is not science fiction—it's history. Earth has already endured five major extinction-level events in the last 500 million years.[208] One such event, proposed by the increasingly supported Younger Dryas Impact

Hypothesis, suggests that a cosmic collision triggered abrupt climate change and mass extinctions just 11,600 years ago—a geological blink of an eye.

Today, we are living through another extinction event—this time, one caused by humans. Human activity—through deforestation, climate change, industrial pollution, overexploitation of resources, and the ever-present risk of nuclear conflict—is pushing countless species toward extinction. Species are vanishing at rates 100 to 1,000 times faster than normal, ecosystems are collapsing, and Earth's stability is deteriorating rapidly.

This is not a distant or hypothetical threat. The last known extinction-level impact occurred just over 11,000 years ago—well within the span of human civilization. In cosmic terms, that was yesterday. We are not immune to planetary-scale catastrophes, whether triggered by celestial forces or by ourselves.

We are living on borrowed time. Earth's history is marked by sudden, devastating resets. If we fail to act—both by preparing for external threats and by correcting our self-destructive behavior—we risk becoming just another layer in the fossil record.

Yet despite this looming danger, our priorities remain badly skewed. In FY 2025, NASA's planetary defense budget—focused on detecting and tracking near-Earth objects (NEOs)—is approximately $296 million, while the U.S. Department of Defense (DoD) is set to spend around $850 billion on weapons procurement and research.[209] This means the military's weapons-related budget is over 2,870 times larger, or roughly 286,900% more than what is allocated to planetary defense. Despite the potential global threat posed by asteroid impacts, funding for NEO detection accounts for less than 0.04% of U.S. military technology spending.

This staggering and unacceptable gap exposes a grave failure of foresight in U.S. congressional priorities, where the focus dangerously leans toward profiting from military exports and fueling the imminent threat of nuclear war—rather than protecting the planet from a deadly space threat in the name of peace.

Section 10: Göbekli Tepe and the Shift to Agriculture

Shortly after the end of the Younger Dryas, around 11,600 years ago (9600 BCE), humans constructed Göbekli Tepe in what is now southeastern Turkey—approximately 7,000 years before the construction of Stonehenge (2500 BCE) by an agriculturally developed society. This discovery challenges the traditional narrative that civilization emerged only after the advent of agriculture. Remarkably, Göbekli Tepe was built not by settled farmers, but by hunter-gatherers.[210]

Adding to the significance of this site, the earliest domesticated wheat was discovered in the nearby Karaçadag Hills, less than twenty miles from Göbekli Tepe.[211] This proximity raises important questions: could the need to feed the builders of such a monumental site—possibly a temple—have spurred the development of agriculture? Large-scale food production would have been necessary to support both the construction and ongoing use of the complex.[212]

Traditionally, it is believed that people first established villages, and only after achieving stability and surplus they built temples or central communal structures. Göbekli Tepe, however, suggests a reversal of this sequence: the temple may have come first, prompting the development of a permanent settlement around it.[213]

The site itself is a massive ceremonial complex composed of intricately carved, T-shaped megalithic pillars arranged in circular formations.[214] Each pillar weighs up to seven tons and stands as tall as sixteen feet. One unfinished pillar, still in the quarry, weighs an estimated fifty tons.[215] The scale and sophistication of Göbekli Tepe suggest that symbolic thought, social organization, and advanced architectural skills existed long before the rise of agriculture—perhaps even paving the way for it.[216]

Section 11: Agricultural Revolution and Rise of Civilization

As the climate stabilized in the Holocene era, which began about 9600 BCE at the end of the last Ice Age (Younger Dryas), conditions favored the rise of agriculture. Human societies began to domesticate plants and animals, shifting from hunting to farming.

The rise of both megalithic architecture and agriculture may not have resulted solely from the independent innovation of hunter-gatherer societies, but rather from the transfer of knowledge by survivors of a lost civilization that existed before the Younger Dryas. These survivors—often referred to as the "bringers of civilization"—are believed to have passed down moral codes, artistic traditions, crafts, and agricultural techniques to early societies.[217]

It is also possible that they imparted architectural and engineering skills to the people of Göbekli Tepe. If these nomadic hunter-gatherers required instruction in such advanced practices, it suggests they had no prior knowledge of them—implying that these seeders of knowledge played a pivotal role in the founding of civilization in the aftermath of a great flood.[218]

The Agricultural Revolution led to permanent settlements, population growth, and increasing social complexity. With more stable food sources, communities developed labor specialization, governance systems, and cultural innovations, setting the stage for urban life.

In contrast, mainstream archaeology maintains that the first established civilizations emerged around 5,000 years ago in regions such as Mesopotamia, Ancient Egypt, the Indus Valley, and Ancient China. According to this view, these organized societies developed gradually and were characterized by cities, writing systems, bureaucracies, and state-level governance.

Section 12: Lost Civilizations Before the Younger Dryas?

Contrary to mainstream archaeology, some alternative archaeologist's propose that an advanced civilization may have existed before the Younger Dryas, only to be destroyed by the abrupt climate shift or a cosmic impact. Common claims include:

- **Atlantis.** Plato describes the lost city of Atlantis as "an island larger than Libya and Asia combined... engulfed by earthquakes" and ultimately destroyed by "the Deluge," and "disappeared in the depths of the sea," dating it to "nine thousand years" before the time of Solon—corresponding to around 11,600 years ago (9600 BCE) in our calendar.[219]

- **Gunung Padang** (Java, Indonesia). Plato's date for the lost continent of Atlantis aligns with the end of the Younger Dryas, when sea levels rose by up to 400 feet (122 meters), submerging much of Sundaland—a vast Southeast Asian landmass. This event transformed highlands into today's Indonesian islands. Some suggest Sundaland could be Atlantis, with Gunung Padang—a possible pyramid dating back 24,000 years—supporting the theory.[220]

- **Baalbek** (Lebanon) and **Puma Punku** (Bolivia). Baalbek features the massive "Temple of Jupiter," built on megalithic foundations with stones estimated to weigh up to 800 tons, possibly dating back over 10,000 years. Puma Punku sits over 12,500 feet above sea level and features precisely cut 100-ton andesite stones with complex interlocking shapes that seem to surpass the capabilities of known ancient cultures.[221, 222]

- **The Younger Dryas Impact Hypothesis.** An "extraterrestrial impact 12,900 years ago that contributed to the megafaunal extinctions and the Younger Dryas cooling," which resulted in catastrophic flooding around the world 11,600 years ago (9600 BCE).[223]

These ideas remain highly controversial and are not widely accepted within the mainstream archaeological and scientific communities.

The dominant academic view holds that human prehistory reflects gradual biological evolution, cognitive development, and cumulative cultural innovation. In this framework, complex societies emerged incrementally from Ice Age hunter-gatherer foundations, without evidence of a lost advanced civilization.

By contrast, Graham Hancock and proponents of the Younger Dryas impact hypothesis, such as Richard Firestone and colleagues, argue that a catastrophic event around 12,800 years ago disrupted or destroyed an earlier, advanced civilization.

In Hancock's interpretation, fragments of this civilization survived and transmitted knowledge that later influenced monumental sites such as Göbekli Tepe and the rise of ancient civilizations. Firestone's position is more narrowly scientific: he proposes that a comet or airburst triggered abrupt climate change and ecological collapse at the onset of the Younger Dryas, though he does not necessarily endorse the existence of a lost global civilization.

CHAPTER 3

Has Human Civilization Progressed?

The question of whether human civilization has progressed over the past 11,600 years is profound, touching not only on our technological achievements but also on our philosophical and cultural development.

In a time marked by rapid technological advancement, global instability, and environmental crisis, this question has become more urgent than ever. Three modern thinkers—Graham Hancock, Neil deGrasse Tyson, and Annie Jacobsen—each offer compelling and provocative perspectives on humanity's past, present, and potential future. While they come from different intellectual disciplines—Hancock from alternative archaeology, Tyson from astrophysics, and Jacobsen from investigative journalism—their works converge on one sobering truth: civilization is far more fragile than we are often willing to admit.

They challenge dominant narratives about human progress and urge us to reexamine not only how we think, but what we think we know. Whether through rediscovering ancient knowledge, adopting a cosmic perspective, or confronting existential threats, all three thinkers call for a radical shift in our understanding of what it means to be human in a precarious world.

Section 1: Graham Hancock—*Magicians of the Gods*

Graham Hancock challenges mainstream academic views and conventional archaeological understanding by proposing that civilization is far older and more advanced than most scholars currently acknowledge. In *Magicians of the Gods,* Hancock argues that an advanced Ice Age civilization existed long before the rise of ancient cultures such as Mesopotamia and Egypt.

He links the collapse of this lost world to a cataclysmic event at the end of the LGP—around 12,800 years ago—during the Younger Dryas. This event, he suggests, triggered massive global flooding and environmental upheaval, effectively erasing a sophisticated culture and plunging humanity into a dark age. For Hancock, modern civilization represents not the first emergence of advanced knowledge, but a second attempt—reconstructed from the fragmented remnants and fading cultural memory of a lost past.

Hancock expands his argument in *America Before*, where he asserts that the Americas played a central role in this forgotten history. Challenging long-standing academic assumptions, he presents archaeological, genetic, and mythological evidence indicating that advanced civilizations may have existed in the Americas far earlier than traditionally accepted. Hancock highlights mound complexes, such as the Serpent Mound; ancient road systems with alignments of astronomical significance; and mythical stories that speak of ancient floods, lost civilizations, and sky-beings, which he interprets as traces of real events.

In developing this narrative, Hancock suggests that humanity's progress has not followed a straight linear path but has instead been shaped by what he terms "amnesia"—a deep and widespread forgetting of our own past.[224] Despite our modern technological advancements, he argues, we remain spiritually and ecologically impoverished, disconnected from the deeper wisdom that once guided earlier civilizations. Modern humanity, in his view, resembles children playing with powerful toys, blind to the long-term consequences. This critique forms a key theme in Hancock's work, where he repeatedly warms against our society's overreliance on materialism and technology, emphasizing that we may be blindly advancing toward another potential collapse.

Rather than viewing history as a steady march of progress, Hancock believes we are trapped in a kind of mental Stone Age—clinging to rigid scientific paradigms, dismissing alternative interpretations, and ignoring ancient warnings, all of which further deepen this state of mental stagnation. For Hancock, rediscovering this lost history is not merely an academic pursuit but a vital step toward reconnecting with a more meaningful and balanced way of life. For him, the ancient past holds not just knowledge but a forgotten form of wisdom, essential for our survival and spiritual renewal.

In the closing chapter of *Magicians of the Gods*, Hancock introduces a bold and provocative idea: that ancient civilizations, destroyed by the Younger Dryas comet impact around 12,800 years ago, attempted to warn future generations through myths, monuments, and astronomical alignments. He connects this ancient catastrophe to what he sees as a potential return event—possibly as soon as the year 2040—and urges modern society to stop wasting its energies on "murderous feuds in the name of 'God,' or 'country,' or political ideology, or selfish greed…"[225] Instead, echoing the perspective of Tyson mentioned later, he advocates for a broader view—one that looks upward to the cosmos, where clues to both our past and future may reside.[226]

Central to Hancock's theory is the belief that a cometary fragment— part of a recurring celestial cycle—was responsible for the Younger Dryas cooling and the accompanying environmental upheaval. He argues that Earth is once again passing through a similar "danger zone," lasting until 2040, based on long-term astronomical rhythms.[227] Although this theory is not accepted by mainstream science, Hancock maintains that ancient cultures recognized these cycles and encoded warnings about them into their structures, stories, and myths in the hope that future civilizations might decipher them in time.

Hancock argues that the year 2030 falls within what he describes as a "window of danger" indicated by the ancient Maya.[228] In his interpretation, this period of risk is derived from his reading of the Maya Long Count calendar, which he believes points to a broader era of upheaval or transformation rather than a single catastrophic date.

The window of danger is not a specific day, but a span of years that he associates with heightened global instability—environmental, geological, or societal—based on his interpretation of cyclical time in the Long Count system. He does not claim that the Maya calendar ends in 2030; instead, he accepts the mainstream view that a major cycle concluded in 2012.[229] However, he reinterprets 2012 not as an endpoint or a failed doomsday prophecy, but as the beginning of an extended period of heightened risk.

In his view, the Maya calendar formed part of an ancient system designed to track recurring celestial cycles, particularly those connected to potential comet impacts. The year 2030, therefore, falls within this broader timeframe—approximately 2012 to 2040—which he believes could bring renewed cosmic threats, possibly culminating in the return of what he calls the "Phoenix" comet around 2040.[230]

Another major piece of evidence Hancock explores is the ancient site of Göbekli Tepe, dated to around 9600 BCE. He argues that the site was not merely a religious or ceremonial center, as is often assumed, but a kind of celestial warning system. The animal carvings and the orientation of the pillars—especially Pillar 43—he suggests, encode advanced astronomical knowledge, particularly about meteor showers such as the Taurids, which he believes may be connected to the original impact event that ended the Ice Age.[231] In this reading, Göbekli Tepe is a deliberate time capsule—a legacy left by survivors to preserve cosmic knowledge for the benefit of future humanity.

Hancock's broader critique centers on modern civilization's preoccupation with itself. He contends that ancient people looked not inward, but upward, to the sky. Their myths, in his interpretation, were not psychological projections of inner states but coded messages about astronomical phenomena. To truly understand our place in the world, Hancock argues, we must recognize our vulnerability to cosmic forces and our deep interconnection with the rhythms of the universe.

This is not, he emphasizes, astrology. It is cosmic memory—real, physical knowledge about celestial cycles passed down through myth, monument, and ritual. Hancock believes that ancient civilizations spent thousands of years carefully observing the sky, tracking dangerous patterns such as comet showers or "precessional" cycles.[232] They then encoded this survival knowledge into their myths, stories, and sacred structures—not as metaphor, but as memory. In this context, Göbekli Tepe becomes a celestial archive, the Mayan calendar a cosmic clock, and myth a vessel for intergenerational warning. The message is clear: our greatest threats—and perhaps our deepest wisdom—may come not from within, but from the stars.

Section 2: Neil deGrasse Tyson—*Starry Messenger*

While Hancock looks to the past for answers, Tyson gazes toward the future, embracing a cosmic perspective—a way of seeing Earth and humanity not as the center of existence, but as a fragile blue dot in an immense universe. Tyson maintains that this shift in perspective "disconnects our ego" and fosters a deeper sense of humility and responsibility for our actions.[233] When we realize how tiny our planet is in the grand scheme of the cosmos, the divisions that separate us—race, borders, politics, ideology—start to seem trivial, even absurd.

In *Starry Messenger*, Tyson offers what he calls a "wake-up call to civilization."[234] Despite tremendous scientific and technological progress, humanity still struggles with basic issues: misinformation, tribalism, and short-term thinking. "People no longer know who or what to trust," he writes. "We've lost all sight of what distinguishes facts from opinions."[235] Instead of focusing on space facts or astrophysical theories, Tyson uses the lens of science and the vastness of the cosmos to explore how we might approach the challenges of the modern world with greater clarity, humility, and reason.[236]

Tyson is not suggesting that science has all the answers to our problems. Rather, he insists that scientific thinking—valuing evidence over belief, reason over rhetoric—provides the best tools for navigating complex social and cultural issues. Tyson claims, "as a species, we might not possess the maturity or wisdom the future requires to assure the survival of civilization."[237] Whether addressing misinformation, inequality, or environmental crisis, Tyson calls for approaching problems with curiosity and encourages us to question assumptions, test hypotheses, and revise our knowledge for understanding—hallmarks of intellectual humility. Scientific thinking helps us distinguish between objective truths, personal beliefs, and political feelings, that is, between what is real and what is merely persuasive.[238]

One of Tyson's central concerns is that although we have the knowledge and tools to address issues like climate change, clean energy, and public health, we frequently fall short due to a lack of will, cooperation, and foresight. Our continued reliance on fossil fuels, for instance, is not a failure of science but of politics and culture.[239] We know what must be done, yet we resist taking action. Tyson challenges us to step outside our "cave door" and broaden our perspective, encouraging us to uncover insights that could solve our "cave problems" through new ways of seeing and doing.[240]

He urges us to reflect on our shared humanity. All humans originated in Africa—the "cradle of mankind"—yet people continue to divide themselves by race, status, and other superficial traits.[241] Many gain a false sense of superiority by comparing themselves to others in wealth, intelligence, or appearance. These distinctions, while socially constructed, often fuel deep and dangerous inequalities.[242] But in the beginning—and in the end—Tyson reminds us, "we're all African."[243]

The genetic differences we use to define and divide ourselves are, in fact, minuscule compared to what we share. All humans share more than 99.9% of their DNA. This reminder of our common origin is not just a scientific observation—it's a moral call to unity and compassion.

This cosmic perspective extends how Tyson views life and death. To our amazement we suddenly exist—after countless millennia of not existing.[244] We often take being alive for granted. Tyson asks, "If you could live forever, would you?" He suggests that there is perhaps "no greater de-motivating force" that would rob life of its value than the knowledge that we will live forever. By contrast, the awareness that we will die one day, however, should be the motivating force that drives us: the urgency to give our lives meaning and leave a lasting mark on the world. For over thirty-five years, I have shared this same conviction with Tyson: "If death gives meaning to life, then to live forever is to live a life with no meaning at all."[245]

Our brief existence—just 75 years—is but a fleeting moment, a heartbeat in the endless flow of time. This reality becomes a reason, not merely to seek personal fulfillment, but to improve the human condition. And if our time is so short, the least we can do is to stop killing one another over differences in belief, identity or worldview.[246] Humans are the only species that routinely kills its own kind, committing over 400,000 homicides a year.[247] Tyson sees this not only as a tragic failure of morality, but as a dangerous misuse of intelligence and agency.

Tyson reflects, "Being alive is the time to celebrate being alive—every waking moment. Along the way, why not strive to make the world a better place today than yesterday, simply for the privilege of having lived in it."[248] He encourages us to "keep looking up ... to become better shepherds of our own civilization," reminding us that each of us is alive against astronomical odds—we each won the lottery only once.[249]

Tyson's *Starry Messenger* is a call to elevate our thinking. He challenges us to be better stewards of the planet and of one another—not through blind optimism, but through reasoned understanding and a shared sense of humanity. His message is clear: If we want to build a more peaceful, sustainable, and compassionate civilization, we must first change how we see ourselves.

Section 3: Annie Jacobsen—*Nuclear War: A Scenario*

While Hancock looks to the past and Tyson gazes toward the future, Jacobsen remains grounded in the present. Annie Jacobsen's *Nuclear War: A Scenario* presents a chilling, minute-by-minute reconstruction of a hypothetical nuclear conflict, illustrating how quickly such a war could escalate into global catastrophe.

The detonation of a 1-megaton thermonuclear weapon begins with a flash of light. The heat instantly reaches a staggering 180 million degrees

Fahrenheit—more than six and a half times hotter than the core of the sun—an intensity that defies human comprehension.[250] If detonated over a city like New York or Seoul, a 1-megaton bomb would kill millions of people in a superheated flash.[251]

By contrast, the most powerful thermonuclear bomb ever detonated was the Tsar Bomba, tested by the Soviet Union in 1961 with a yield of 50 megatons. This is equivalent to the explosive force of more than 3,300 Hiroshima bombs detonating simultaneously. At detonation, the flash of light reached a temperature of approximately 540 million degrees Fahrenheit—about twenty times hotter than the core of the Sun.

Structured in three tense, 24-minute "acts," Jacobsen's narrative in *Nuclear War: A Scenario* illustrates how civilization could collapse within hours—echoing warnings from military leaders like former STRATCOM commander General Kehler, who has stated that nuclear war could end life on Earth in just two hours.[252]

In her narrative, Jacobsen critiques the concept of nuclear "deterrence," a strategy introduced by the U.S. Defense Department in the 1950s, which was claimed to safeguard the world from nuclear war.[253] One of the most alarming issues she examines is the decades-old "launch on warning" policy, also known as "hair-trigger alert," which gives world leaders mere minutes to decide whether to retaliate—often based on incomplete or faulty information. Decades later, we are still on a "high-alert, hair-trigger" status."[254] She challenges the Mutual Assured Destruction (MAD) theory, arguing it is dangerously dependent on rational actors, flawless technology, and seamless communication.[255]

The long-term consequences of this devastation are unimaginable: a nuclear winter plunging global temperatures, wiping out agriculture, and leading to widespread starvation; radiation poisoning, ozone depletion, and harmful ultraviolet exposure destroying entire species; and massive outbreaks of insect-borne diseases and epidemics, as humans struggle at the edge of extinction.[256] More than "5 billion people could die" in a nuclear war—not directly from the initial blast itself, but from the prolonged effects of nuclear winter, famine, and societal collapse.[257]

Jacobsen echoes Khrushechev's chilling warning: "The survivors will envy the dead."[258] The recovery of life would take an estimated 24,000 years—roughly twice as long as it took for humans to evolve from hunter-gatherers to the modern era.[259] Her core message is stark: nuclear weapons themselves are the enemy—not Russia, not North Korea.[260]

Yet amid this bleak outlook, Jacobsen finds fragments of hope. Like Hancock, who turns to archaeology for insight, she looks to the remnants of Göbekli Tepe—a 12,000-year-old site that has preserved traces of human emotion, intention, and connection.[261] Then, an unknown catastrophe suddenly brought about their end. No living quarters have been discovered—no cemeteries, no human remains.

Jacobsen suggests that this was not a natural disaster—such as an earthquake, meteor, or flood—but possibly something human-made.[262] While she does not explicitly propose a nuclear explosion, the reference to a swift, dramatic end, along with the dismissal of natural causes, leaves room for that possibility. If we entertain the idea of a nuclear explosion, it might imply the existence of an advanced civilization or technology—perhaps something beyond our current understanding—that led to their downfall. She reflects: "What happened at Göbekli Tepe? What caused these humans to suddenly meet their end?"[263]

Drawing a parallel to our own uncertain future, Jacobsen imagines a time millennia after a potential nuclear apocalypse, when future generations might uncover the remnants of our civilization. In this distant future, they, too, might ask: Who were these people? How did they fall? What happened to them?[264] This reflection evokes a quiet optimism—that even in the face of disaster, the human capacity for hope and resilience may endure, preserved in the traces we leave behind.

Jacobsen also advocates for dialogue over conflict, emphasizing that the true progress of civilization may depend not on military power, but on communication and mutual understanding. In an interview with Lex Fridman, she shares a deeply human sentiment that resonates with many of us: "Ultimately, when you think about the long arc of time and human civilization, it does kind of make you want to communicate more with your enemies, with your adversaries."[265]

To underscore the fragility of civilization's progress, Jacobsen invokes Albert Einstein's famous warning: "I know not with what weapons World War III will be fought, but World War IV will be fought with sticks and stones."[266] This highlights the precarious nature of human advancement—suggesting that all the wisdom, technology, and history we've accumulated could be wiped out in an instant.

Yet there remains a persistent spark of humanity that survives even in the face of such devastation—an enduring hope in the fragments of our past and in our capacity for communication and empathy.

The ultimate takeaway, however, is a humbling reminder: in the face of existential threats, the achievements of civilization could dissolve into myth, leaving future generations to ponder what was lost and, perhaps, rediscover what was once buried. Jacobsen's message is blunt: our civilization could end not gradually, but all at once.

Section 4: Comparative Perspectives

Graham Hancock, Neil deGrasse Tyson, and Annie Jacobsen all question mainstream or widely accepted ways of thinking, showing that mistaken or unexamined assumptions—whether in history, science, or society—can threaten human progress and even our survival.

Hancock critiques academic institutions, particularly in archaeology, for dismissing evidence that contradicts accepted timelines—an attitude he attributes to intellectual arrogance and fear of paradigm shifts. Tyson focuses on a broader cultural issue: society's preference for belief over evidence. He argues that only through the scientific method—curiosity, humility, and critical thinking—can we address global crises like climate change and misinformation. Jacobsen exposes systemic failures in nuclear policy, warning that policies like MAD rely on fallible humans making rapid decisions under uncertain conditions.

Despite their differing perspectives—historical, scientific, and geopolitical—all three emphasize the urgent need to rethink our assumptions and take meaningful action.

Section 5: Similarities of Perspectives

One of the most prominent themes across the works of Hancock, Tyson, and Jacobsen is the fragility of human civilization. Each, in their own way, questions the stability and longevity of human progress in the face of catastrophe, poor decision-making, and narrow worldviews. All three challenge conventional narratives about human progress and object to the way humanity thinks and makes decisions.

Hancock argues that an ancient, advanced civilization may have existed long before the rise of known cultures like Mesopotamia or Egypt, only to be obliterated by a cataclysmic event at the end of the last Ice Age. In his view, this lost civilization's sudden disappearance left humanity in a dark age, which persisted until the re-emergence of modern cultures. He calls for a reevaluation of history, arguing that mainstream archaeology overlooks evidence of lost civilizations. Hancock's theory that there may have been an advanced civilization long before what mainstream archaeology recognizes disrupts the linear progression of human history. He criticizes the archaeological establishment for being dismissive of unorthodox ideas and ignoring evidence that doesn't fit the mainstream narrative.

Tyson emphasizes the contrast between the technological advancements that have shaped our lives—such as the invention of the automobile, airplane, nuclear weapons, the World Wide Web, and smartphones, along with space exploration in the 20th and 21st centuries—and the ongoing social and political failures that continue to afflict humanity, warning that despite our technological progress, we remain socially and politically immature. He encourages adopting a cosmic perspective to rethink humanity's place in the universe, suggesting that such a shift could help us reassess our priorities. Tyson laments the preference for political rhetoric over scientific reasoning and emphasizes the need for intellectual humility as essential for solving global problems.

Jacobsen, though focusing more specifically on the existential threat of nuclear war, offers a chilling reflection on how humanity's progress could be wiped out in a matter of hours, underscoring the fragility of our achievements. She contends that nuclear warfare presents a unique existential threat that could quickly unravel modern civilization, challenging the belief that humanity's advancements are immune to destruction. Jacobsen warns of the irrational decision-making embedded in nuclear deterrence strategies, underscoring how easily high-stakes misjudgments could unravel civilization.

Together, these perspectives reveal a common concern: humanity's unwillingness to confront truths—whether in history, politics, or global security. This intellectual and moral shortfall, they argue, threatens the advancement of knowledge and risks undoing the very progress we pride ourselves on.

Section 6: Differences of Perspectives

Though united by a concern for humanity's future, Hancock, Tyson, and Jacobsen offer distinctly different interpretations of our civilization's trajectory.

Hancock looks to the distant past, arguing that modern society has lost not only historical knowledge but also spiritual and ecological wisdom—ways of living that may have helped early civilizations to exist in harmony with the Earth. He draws on architectural mysteries, mythological narratives, and oral traditions to suggest the existence of a forgotten culture far older than mainstream archaeology acknowledges. His tone is both tragic and reverent: tragic for what has been lost, and reverent toward the ancient survivors who preserved fragments of their knowledge for future generations.

Tyson, by contrast, turns his gaze outward and forward. Through his concept of the cosmic perspective, he invites us to see Earth not as the center of the universe, but as a fragile speck in a vast, indifferent cosmos. This shift in viewpoint, he argues, can help dissolve human divisions—national, racial, ideological—and promote a deeper sense of unity and responsibility. Tyson is less concerned with what we've lost and more focused on what we might gain: a future guided by science, reason, and shared planetary stewardship.

Jacobsen centers her analysis on the precarious present and the looming threats of the near future. Her work is grounded in the real-world mechanics of destruction—nuclear protocols, defense systems, radiation impacts, and the potential onset of nuclear winter. Drawing from military insiders, scientific experts, and declassified materials, Jacobsen offers a sobering portrayal of how swiftly civilization could unravel. Her tone is urgent, at times bleak, yet she finds a glimmer of hope in human empathy, memory, and communication. For her, the path to survival lies not in grand narratives but in honest dialogue and emotional awareness.

Together, these three thinkers offer a broad and contrasting spectrum: from ancient echoes to cosmic visions to present-day alarms—each framing human civilization through a distinct lens of loss, possibility, or peril.

Section 7: Three Perspectives, One Urgent Message

Though Hancock, Tyson, and Jacobsen differ in their tone, methods, and focus, their work converges on a crucial insight: the survival of human civilization depends on how we think—and how we change. Hancock invites us to rediscover lost wisdom and reframe our understanding of history. Tyson urges us to adopt a broader, cosmic perspective grounded in reason and science. Jacobsen demands that we reckon with the very real threats we've created for ourselves and act decisively to avert disaster.

Together, their perspectives form a triad of warning and hope. Hancock reminds us that civilizations can—and have—disappeared. Tyson shows us that humanity can still evolve, not biologically, but intellectually. Jacobsen warns that even the most advanced society is only minutes away from self-destruction.

In a world increasingly shaped by complexity, crisis, and uncertainty, these thinkers challenge us to move beyond complacency. Whether by looking to the past, the stars, or the ticking clock of nuclear tension, they agree on one thing: what we do now matters immensely.

Section 8: The Kardashev Scale

Nikolai S. Kardashev was a Russian astrophysicist and radio astronomer best known for introducing the Kardashev Scale in 1964, a theoretical framework designed to measure a civilization's level of technological advancement based on its energy consumption. In his seminal paper, "Transmission of Information by Extraterrestrial Civilizations," Kardashev proposed a scale that categorized civilizations according to the amount of energy they can harness and utilize.[267]

At the base of the scale, a Type I civilization utilizes all the solar energy available on its planet. A Type II civilization utilizes the total energy output of its star. A Type III civilization harnesses the energy of an entire galaxy and likely possesses interstellar travel capabilities.[268]

Though not included in Kardashev's classification, modern theorists often refer to Earth's current state as Type 0—a civilization that has not yet achieved full planetary energy utilization. Some modern theorists, such as Michio Kaku, calculate Earth to be roughly Type 0.7 on the Kardashev Scale, based on current global energy consumption—still largely dependent on fossil fuels and far from utilizing the planet's full energy potential.[269] According to Kaku, Earth is approximately one to two centuries away from becoming a Type I civilization, a few thousand years away from reaching a Type II civilization, and anywhere from one hundred thousand to one million years away from achieving a Type III civilization.[270] For now, we're just cavemen with Wi-Fi.

Kardashev's scale has since become a concept in discussions about the future of human civilization, extraterrestrial life, and the long-term prospects of space exploration. It provides a framework for imagining civilizations far more advanced than our own.

When compared to the potential of Type I, II, or III civilizations, humanity's current stage of development reveals a sobering reality. Despite millennia of progress, our species has made limited strides in terms of energy harnessing. Instead, much of our technological advancement has been directed toward self-destructive capabilities, particularly in the development of weapons of mass destruction.

In the 11,600 years since the dawn of civilization—or perhaps since our second or even third chance at existence—we remain a species still struggling with the very basics of planetary responsibility.

Section 9: Closing Reflection

Even with our incredible technological feats—sending robotic explorers to Mars, decoding the human genome, and developing groundbreaking medical treatments—much of the world still operates using outdated systems. We're still confined to the ground, living in houses—whether modest or extravagant—that resemble modern-day versions of caves, rather than in gravity-defying homes suspended in the sky, with transparent walls and panoramic views.

Our transportation has stagnated. Our vehicles are still saddled with gasoline-dependent combustion engines. Whether you're driving a basic economy car or a high-end sports car, you're still in a metal coffin on wheels. Instead of zipping through the skies in advanced flying vehicles, we're stuck navigating the same old roadways. We haven't even reached the world imagined by *The Jetsons*.

Despite breakthroughs in technology, we continue to rely on fossil fuels—remnants of ancient life—while neglecting the vast potential of renewable energy sources like solar or fusion power. And although our technology has made significant leaps, our behavior often remains anchored in the same primitive instincts that shaped us millennia ago.

Why, after all these years, does society still rely so heavily on fossil fuels? With all the innovation happening in energy and transportation, it's baffling that revolutionary solutions—such as water-powered vehicles—haven't become the norm. Some suggest it's not a lack of ingenuity, but the deliberate suppression of these technologies. There are persistent rumors of inventors whose breakthrough energy solutions were buried and their patents seized under mysterious or even deadly circumstances.

Could it be that a conspiracy of elites—corporations, shadow governments, and covert organizations operating from secretive underground bases—are actively stifling innovation to maintain control over the world's resources? Are these forces keeping advanced technologies under wraps, holding humanity back from a true technological renaissance?

This raises profound historical questions: Why did it take humanity nearly 2,000 years after the classical era to rediscover and harness electricity? Why wasn't the transistor—central to all modern electronics—conceived centuries ago? And why, despite the concept of the electric battery being known for millennia (the so-called Baghdad Battery), has it taken so long to develop it into a viable tool for reshaping our energy systems?[271]

What economic, political, and ideological forces are preventing us from entering a new era of abundance, sustainability, and freedom? Are we being held back in a metaphorical Stone Age, clinging to outdated systems that primarily serve the interests of the few, while the majority continue to suffer? Could we already be living in a utopia if these invisible barriers were removed? Or is the sluggish pace of our advancement simply the result of our collective, slow evolution?

While civilization has undoubtedly made strides in certain areas, in many others, it has remained largely unchanged for the past 11,600 years. Until we transcend our primitive tribal instincts and embrace true global cooperation, ecological responsibility, and spiritual maturity, we risk remaining in the Stone Age—but with more sophisticated gadgets.

CHAPTER 4
The Moon

The Moon is weird. It has long captivated humanity—as a celestial body, a cultural symbol, and a scientific mystery.

Three distinct perspectives on the Moon are considered. *The Book of the Moon* by Rick Stroud presents a scientific and historically grounded account, drawing on astronomy, history, and mythology. *Who Built the Moon?* by Christopher Knight and Alan Butler explores a more speculative idea, proposing the radical hypothesis that the Moon may be an artificial construct. The YouTube channel *The Why Files*, hosted by A.J. Gentile, examines the Moon from a geological perspective, with particular attention to irregularities in the lunar rock and soil samples returned by the Apollo missions. Together, these varied perspectives offer a compelling lens through which to understand how the same celestial object can inspire awe, curiosity, and debate—whether through science, speculation, or geology.

Section 1: Stroud—*The Book of the Moon*

Rick Stroud's *The Book of the Moon* presents an expansive and wide-ranging study of Earth's natural satellite. Blending scientific research with mythology, cultural history, and mystical traditions, Stroud adopts an encyclopedic approach. While he gives space to alternative and controversial ideas, he consistently situates them within historical and cultural frameworks rather than treating them as scientific rivals. The result is a work that seeks to balance wonder with evidence-based inquiry.

Stroud grounds his discussion of lunar origins in the widely accepted Giant Impact Theory, first formalized in 1975 following insights from the Apollo missions.[272] This model proposes that the Moon formed from debris produced by a collision between early Earth and a Mars-sized body billions of years ago.[273] He presents this explanation as the prevailing scientific consensus, carefully avoiding speculative departures.

Although Rick Stroud occasionally addresses controversial or pseudoscientific claims, he does so with clear contextual framing rather than endorsement. In *The Book of the Moon*, a substantial forty-page chapter is devoted to themes such as magic, the occult, astrology, alchemy, and superstition. Rather than presenting these traditions as scientific alternatives, Stroud treats them as culturally and historically significant expressions of humanity's attempt to understand the Moon.[274]

Near the book's conclusion, Stroud turns to the moon-landing controversy, outlining the principal claims of skeptics alongside the scientific and historical evidence that refutes them. In doing so, he maintains a measured tone, presenting competing assertions but ultimately reinforcing the credibility of documented lunar exploration.[275]

One of the book's most intriguing discussions involves seismic experiments conducted during the Apollo missions. Stroud recounts the famous description that the Moon "rang like a bell," a phrase associated with the Apollo 12 mission when NASA deliberately crashed the Lunar Module's ascent stage into the Moon at approximately 3,759 mph, producing a crater roughly 30 feet wide.[276, 277] Seismometers recorded vibrations that built gradually over 7–8 minutes, peaked, and diminished slowly over nearly an hour.[278] Even after 55 minutes, faint reverberations persisted.[279]

Maurice Ewing, co-head of the experiment, famously remarked that it was "as though one had struck a bell."[280] Remarkably, the Moon continued "ringing" for another 25 minutes after his statement.[281] Notably, Stroud does not entertain the speculative "hollow Moon" hypothesis sometimes associated with this poetic phrase. Instead, he allows the seismic anomaly to stand as an example of how unfamiliar data can inspire dramatic metaphors.

However, Stroud limits his discussion primarily to Apollo 12. He does not explore in detail other impact experiments, such as the Apollo 13 S-IVB stage crash. At the time of impact, the stage weighed 30,700 pounds and was traveling at a speed of approximately 5,600 miles per hour.[282] The impact released energy equivalent to 7.7 tons of TNT and generated seismic waves that were first detected 28.4 seconds after the collision.[283] These vibrations continued for three hours and twenty minutes, with a peak amplitude eight times greater than that recorded from the Apollo 12 ascent-stage impact, which had released energy equivalent to 1 ton of TNT.[284]

These broader datasets contribute significantly to modern understanding of the Moon's internal composition, suggesting a dry, fractured interior that transmits seismic waves differently from Earth. Stroud's selectivity does not undermine his argument, but readers seeking a comprehensive technical survey of lunar seismology may find the treatment somewhat limited.

Stroud devotes considerable attention to the biological tide theory—the longstanding belief that the Moon influences human behavior due to its gravitational pull on bodily fluids.[285] Dating back to ancient Greece, this theory holds that the Moon's gravitational pull significantly affects water, and since the average human adult is about 60% water, it must exert influence on people as well—potentially causing headaches, mood swings, or even violent behavior.[286] The term "lunatic" arose from this belief and shaped the way lawmakers framed the Lunacy Act of 1845, affecting how mental illness was legally defined and regulated.[287]

Stroud evaluates the biological tide theory by comparing scales: while the Moon moves 352 quintillion gallons (1.33 sextillion liters) of loosely contained ocean water spread across vast distances, its gravitational pull on the human body is negligible. He cites calculations suggesting the Moon's effect on bodily water is about 1 part in 30 trillion, and its influence on blood is only about 3 parts per million—roughly 0.01 ounces in a 200-pound person.[288] His conclusion is that the Moon's effect on bodily water is far too weak to produce meaningful physiological or psychological changes.

The book, however, provides limited sourcing or endnotes for these numerical claims, making independent verification difficult. Even so, the Lunacy Act 1845 occurred when the world population was about 1.2–1.5 billion; today it exceeds 8.5 billion. Collectively, humanity contains about 94 billion gallons (356 billion liters) of water, yet this still does not make lunar effects on human behavior significant. Unlike oceans, water in the human body is confined within tissues and cells. Modern studies have found little or no consistent evidence linking lunar phases to mental illness, crime, sleep disruption, or unusual behavior.

Some important scientific topics receive only brief mention or are omitted. For example, Stroud does not fully explain why the Moon always shows the same face to Earth. This phenomenon—known as synchronous rotation—occurs because the Moon rotates once every 27.3 days, the same time it takes to orbit Earth. The result is a stable near side and a permanently hidden far side, creating the illusion that the Moon does not rotate at all.[289]

Additionally, Stroud does not delve deeply into certain structural asymmetries. The far-side crust is approximately 12 miles thicker than the near side, and many lunar impact craters exhibit relatively consistent depth-to-diameter ratios, suggesting structural layering beneath the regolith. These features are not mysterious within planetary science, but they represent important aspects of lunar geology that could have enriched the book's scientific depth.

Stroud briefly references a time when Earth existed before it "acquired" a Moon but does not elaborate.[290] Modern planetary science suggests that the Moon plays a stabilizing role in maintaining Earth's axial tilt (obliquity). Without this stabilizing influence, Earth's climate might fluctuate far more dramatically over geological timescales.[291] A fuller exploration would have deepened readers' understanding of the Moon's long-term influence on terrestrial life.

The Book of the Moon succeeds as a broad, culturally informed exploration of humanity's relationship with its nearest celestial neighbor. Stroud maintains a generally evidence-based approach, especially concerning lunar formation and seismic experimentation. He acknowledges myths, occult traditions, and speculative interpretations but frames them historically rather than endorsing them.

At the same time, certain technical topics—such as the full scope of Apollo seismic data, lunar crustal asymmetry, and Earth-Moon dynamical evolution—receive limited attention. The absence of detailed endnotes in some sections may also frustrate readers seeking deeper scientific verification.

Nevertheless, Stroud achieves a careful balance: he preserves the Moon's aura of mystery while grounding his narrative in established science. The book invites curiosity and reflection, encouraging readers to appreciate both the cultural symbolism and the empirical reality of the Moon—an object of wonder, examined with disciplined restraint.

Section 2: Knight and Butler—*Who Built the Moon?*

Christopher Knight and Alan Butler's *Who Built the Moon?* presents a highly unorthodox and speculative theory: that the Moon is not a naturally occurring celestial body, but an artificial construct—engineered and positioned in Earth's orbit with the specific purpose of enabling life to exist on our planet.[292]

The authors argue that the Moon's size, distance from Earth, and alignment with the Sun produce such mathematically precise relationships that they cannot be the result of random cosmic events. Instead, they interpret these characteristics as the signature of intelligent design— possibly by extraterrestrials or even future humans.

Who Built the Moon? begins by examining the unique features of the Earth–Moon–Sun system. Knight and Butler, citing Isaac Asimov, highlight what he describes as "the most unlikely coincidence imaginable": the fact that the Moon is approximately 400 times smaller than the Sun but also about 400 times closer to Earth—making both appear the same size in the sky.[293, 294] This precise ratio allows for total solar eclipses, an event that is not known to occur in any other known planetary system. They also highlight the Moon's stabilizing effect on Earth's axial tilt, which is essential to maintaining a climate suitable for life.

Challenging mainstream scientific theories, Knight and Butler take aim at the widely accepted Giant Impact Hypothesis, which proposes that the Moon formed from debris after a collision between Earth and a Mars-sized body. They argue that this theory fails to adequately explain the Moon's specific orbital mechanics, relatively low density, and unusual chemical composition.[295]

The authors also reference data from the Apollo missions, specifically seismic readings recorded when lunar modules and other spacecraft components were intentionally crashed into the Moon's surface. In November 1969, for instance, the Apollo 12 crew deliberately crashed their lunar module into the Moon after it separated from the command module while orbiting during their return to Earth. The impact, equivalent to one ton of TNT, caused seismic reverberations that lasted nearly an hour.[296, 297]

Building on this experiment, the Apollo 13 mission in April 1970 involved crashing an even larger and heavier object—the Saturn V rocket booster—into the Moon. Knight and Butler maintain that this impact, equivalent to 11.5 tons of TNT, penetrated to a depth of 25 miles and produced reverberations that continued for more than 3 hours and 20 minutes.[298] However, NASA's *Apollo 13 Mission Report* (September 1970) indicates the impact was equivalent to "7.7 tons of TNT" instead of 11.5 tons, and that the reverberations lasted "over 4 hours" (as previously noted).[299] These surprisingly long-lasting vibrations led some scientists to conclude that the Moon may have an unusually light core—or perhaps no core at all.[300]

This unusual seismic response gave rise to descriptions of the Moon "ringing like a bell," which Knight and Butler interpreted as potential evidence that the Moon is hollow, or at least far less dense than prevailing models suggest—an interpretation associated with the Hollow Moon Theory. They argue this supports the idea of artificial construction.[301]

A key part of their argument is the use of ancient measurement systems. The authors discuss the "Megalithic Yard," which they claim ancient civilizations used to build astronomical structures such as Stonehenge.[302] They argue that the system encodes precise Earth–Moon–Sun relationships, including ratios of distance, size, and angular measurements. As they put it:

> We found that these early Megalithic builders viewed a circle as having 366 degrees rather than the 360 degrees that we use today. We realized that there really should be 366 degrees in a circle for the very good reason that there are 366 rotations of the Earth in one orbit of the Sun.[303]

These relationships, they claim, often result in simple, whole-number values when calculated using the Megalithic Yard—suggesting that prehistoric societies may have inherited knowledge of a cosmic design.

In the second-to-last chapter, Knight and Butler introduce the "Möbius Principle," named after mathematician August Ferdinand Möbius. The concept draws on the Möbius strip—a surface with only one side and one edge that challenges conventional ideas about dimension and geometry.[304] Beyond mathematics, the strip appears in engineering applications such as conveyor belts and electronic components, and in art it symbolizes infinity, paradox, and the unity of opposites.

In *Who Built the Moon?*, Knight and Butler use this image as a metaphor for time loops and self-creating systems—a structure in which inside and outside become indistinguishable. Through the Möbius Principle, they propose a non-linear model of causality in which future events can influence the past. Within this speculative framework, they suggest that future humans—or some advanced intelligence—may have placed the Moon in orbit to ensure the emergence of life and consciousness.[305] The result is a cosmic feedback loop: intelligent life is both the product of the conditions that made it possible and the agent responsible for creating those very conditions.

Roland Emmerich's 2022 sci-fi disaster film *Moonfall*, starring Halle Berry, Patrick Wilson, and John Bradley, follows a disgraced astronaut and a conspiracy theorist who discover that the Moon is a massive alien-built megastructure. When it falls out of orbit and threatens Earth, they learn it was created by ancient human ancestors to preserve life after a war with rogue artificial intelligence.

This central idea closely mirrors the speculative theory in Knight and Butler's 2005 book *Who Built the Moon?*, which argues that the Moon may be an artificial construct placed to support life on Earth. *Moonfall* echoes several of the book's claims, including that the Moon is about 400 times smaller than the Sun but also about 400 times closer to Earth—producing perfect solar eclipses—and that lunar modules intentionally crashed into the Moon caused it to "ring like a bell," suggesting a hollow interior.

Both the film and the book explore the provocative notion that the Moon's origin is not a cosmic accident but rather a deliberate act of advanced intelligence. In this sense, *Moonfall* feels like a cinematic interpretation of the book's core ideas, even though it is not a direct adaptation.

This thematic convergence highlights the speculative basis of *Who Built the Moon?*, which draws heavily on alternative scientific interpretations—most notably the research of Alexander Thom, the Scottish engineer and archaeoastronomer.[306] His work on ancient measurement systems is central to the book's broader argument that the Moon is hollow and artificially constructed.

In their final chapter, "The Möbius Mission," Knight and Butler call for interdisciplinary research to re-examine ancient knowledge, unexplained numerical patterns, and the possibility that cosmic structures like the Moon carry intentional messages or functions.[307] They argue that modern science has become overly compartmentalized and dismissive of anomalies that do not fit established theories, and they advocate a more integrative approach to understanding the universe and humanity's place within it.[308]

Knight and Butler also engage with broader metaphysical questions, including the origins of life and the nature of consciousness. They discuss the complexity of DNA, referencing the Miller–Urey experiment to argue that life's emergence appears too finely tuned to be purely accidental.[309] They suggest that the Moon may be part of a larger, intelligently designed system intended to foster life—not just physically, but potentially spiritually or evolutionarily as well.

The book touches briefly on theological concerns, questioning traditional concepts of God in light of suffering, natural disasters, and what they see as more rational, observable forms of design encoded in nature and the cosmos.[310] They argue that the ancient Megalithic system provides a more objective and measurable "key" to understanding whatever force or intelligence may lie behind the Moon's existence.[311]

Who Built the Moon? is a speculative work that falls short of the empirical standards typical of mainstream scientific literature, yet it stands out as an intriguing piece of alternative cosmology. Knight and Butler provide limited references—some without specific page numbers—and offer no conclusive evidence to support their claims. Instead, they highlight patterns, coincidences, and philosophical questions designed to challenge conventional perspectives.

Regardless of whether one agrees with their conclusions, the book prompts readers to reconsider long-standing assumptions about the Moon, the origins of life, and the possibility that our existence is part of a larger, intelligible cosmic design.

Section 3: Gentile—*The Why Files*

A.J. Gentile has hosted the YouTube channel *The Why Files* since it launched in September 2020, a channel covering mysteries, myths, legends and conspiracies. In an episode titled "The Moon Revealed," Gentile notes that one of the most intriguing Apollo discoveries was that the Moon's surface layer of dust and broken rock appeared older than the layers beneath it.[312] Unlike Earth, where younger rocks lie on the surface, the Moon shows inverted stratigraphy with older soil above younger rocks. Adding to the mystery, the lunar surface is rich in rare, high-strength metals that are scarce on Earth.[313]

From a scientific standpoint, in *The Book of the Moon,* Stroud explains that the top layer of the lunar surface, known as regolith, is older because it has been exposed to meteor bombardment for billions of years.[314] Beneath the regolith lies the megaregolith, which he describes as a younger layer—though he does not satisfactorily explain why the surface layer is considered older than the layer beneath it.[315] On a more speculative note, in *Who Built the Moon?,* Knight and Butler refer only to the Moon rocks brought back by the Apollo missions, using this evidence to cast doubt on the Giant Impact Hypothesis and the idea that the Moon shares a common origin with Earth, but they do not explain how.[316]

Despite the remarkable achievement of landing on the Moon in 1969 and returning with rock and soil samples, the Apollo missions raised more questions than they answered. A.J. Gentile draws attention to, rather than confirms, expectations about lunar formation, as the data reveal numerous inconsistencies that challenge our understanding of Earth's Moon.[317]

One of the more controversial yet persistent theories, as Gentile mentions, is that the Moon may not be a naturally formed object at all, based on its geological and internal structure and chemical properties. To support this claim, Gentile identifies at least seven anomalies that, taken together, challenge conventional explanations.

First, the Moon's geological structure presents an immediate puzzle. On Earth, younger rocks typically form closer to the surface, while older material lies deeper underground. On the Moon, however, this order is reversed. As previously mentioned, Stroud offers an explanation—but not a convincing one. Gentile underscores that lunar surface soils often date back further than the rocks beneath them—a pattern typically seen on Earth only in areas disturbed by excavation or mining.[318] Yet on the Moon, this inversion is widespread.

Second, the Moon's internal structure is equally unusual. In most planetary bodies, heavier materials sink toward the core. Gentile remarks, however, that on the Moon denser materials appear to reside near the surface, with lighter ones at the center—hinting at a shell-like or even hollow interior.[319] Seismic readings from Apollo missions, Gentile says, reinforce this possibility: when parts of the lunar module were crashed into the surface, the Moon reverberated for hours, leading NASA scientists to describe it as "ringing like a bell."[320] He further stresses that seismic waves accelerated at depths of around 40 miles—opposite of what would normally be expected in a typical planetary body—suggesting the presence of a lightweight or hollow layer beneath the crust.[321]

Third, chemical analysis adds another layer of intrigue. Gentile points out that lunar soil contains high concentrations of rare, high-performance metals such as titanium, chromium, and zirconium—elements that are uncommon on Earth and typically used in high-tech applications due to their strength and resistance to heat and corrosion.[322] These metals, he says, are not evenly distributed but are found in specific regions, almost as if placed intentionally.[323] Additionally, Gentile notes the presence of isotopes such as uranium-236 and neptunium-237—materials that do not occur naturally and are byproducts of nuclear reactions.[324] Their presence on the Moon, he argues, is difficult to reconcile with standard geological theories.

Fourth, magnetic anomalies further complicate the picture. Gentile highlights that while the Moon no longer possesses a global magnetic field, many lunar rocks returned by Apollo missions were found to be magnetized. This is difficult to explain, since significant magnetization generally requires a strong magnetic field to be present during the rock's formation.[325]

Fifth, the Moon's age presents another paradox. Some lunar rocks have been dated at over 4.5 billion years—placing them at the very beginning of the solar system and, in some cases, appearing older than Earth's oldest rocks. Gentile argues that if the Earth and Moon formed simultaneously from a common event—as the widely accepted Giant Impact Hypothesis proposes—this discrepancy in age becomes difficult to explain.[326]

Sixth, the Moon's orbit and size further deepen the mystery. Its orbit is nearly perfectly circular—unusual for a natural satellite—and its size-to-distance ratio allows it to perfectly eclipse the Sun from Earth's perspective. This creates the rare phenomenon of total solar eclipses, in which the Sun and Moon appear exactly the same size in the sky. Like Knight and Butler, Gentile concedes that, given the Sun is roughly 400 times larger than the Moon but also about 400 times farther away, this exact match seems statistically improbable.[327]

Finally, as previously noted, Gentile points out that the Moon is unusually large in relation to Earth—approximately one-quarter of Earth's diameter—a proportion unparalleled among known planetary moons. In this respect, the Moon resembles a twin planet more than a typical satellite. Taken together, these characteristics raise profound questions about whether the Moon's orbit and dimensions are merely coincidental—or perhaps deliberately engineered.

Some researchers, Gentile remarks, have proposed a connection between these lunar anomalies and major Earth events—particularly the Younger Dryas, a sudden global cooling period that occurred approximately 12,800 years ago.[328] This era, as previously mentioned, was marked by dramatic climate shifts, widespread extinctions of large animals, and the abrupt collapse of early human cultures. While the cause remains debated, many scientists point to a cosmic impact event, such as a fragmented comet or asteroid. Strikingly, this event coincides with global myths of fire in the sky, great floods, and celestial upheaval.[329]

These myths are widespread, appearing in cultures from Mesopotamia to the Americas. They often describe stars falling, skies darkening, and oceans rising. Some theorists, Gentile notes, suggest that these accounts may reflect real events—possibly tied to a cosmic disturbance involving the Moon.[330] Even more intriguing, he says, are references from ancient cultures that mention a time before the Moon appeared in the sky.[331] Ancient Greek and Roman authors, including Aristotle and Apollonius of Rhodes, refer to the Proselenes—an Arcadian people who claimed to have lived before the Moon's arrival.[332] Similar stories emerge from the

Tiwanaku civilization in Bolivia. Gentile suggests that, if these accounts are more than metaphorical, they may point to a period in human memory when the Moon was a new presence in the sky—whether it appeared millions of years ago or arrived prior to the Younger Dryas.[333]

In 1970, Soviet scientists Mikhail Vasin and Alexander Shcherbakov published a provocative paper titled "Is the Moon the Creation of Intelligence?"[334] They advanced the bold hypothesis that the Moon might be an artificial satellite deliberately placed into Earth's orbit by intelligent beings—perhaps as long as two billion years ago, or even at a time predating our own planet.[335]

According to Vasin and Shcherbakov, the Moon did not originate near Earth but may have come from far beyond it, possibly even from outside our solar system.[336] They argued that it would be extremely difficult for Earth's gravity to naturally capture an object into such a close, nearly circular orbit. In addition to this orbital anomaly, they pointed to unusual aspects of lunar geology, including the presence of rare metals such as chromium, titanium, and zirconium—elements known for their exceptional heat resistance and structural strength.[337] To them, these characteristics suggested the possibility of a durable outer shell rather than a purely natural formation.

Building on these physical and chemical irregularities, Vasin and Shcherbakov ultimately speculated that the Moon might be a colossal "ancient spaceship," engineered by an advanced civilization and later placed in orbit around Earth.[338] They suggested that some form of life may once have existed within it but had since become extinct, leaving the "craft abandoned" and operating automatically.[339] They further proposed that advanced civilizations need not inhabit planetary surfaces and that the interior of a celestial body could serve as a viable habitat.[340] Although highly speculative, their theory aimed to account for what they viewed as the Moon's physical, chemical, and historical anomalies.

If there is any truth to such theories, the implications are profound. The Moon—long seen as a passive, familiar companion—may have played an active role in shaping Earth's history. Whether natural, artificial, or something in between, the Moon remains far stranger than we once believed. Its anomalies challenge conventional models and invite us to reconsider what we know about our planet, the solar system, and the possibility of intelligent life beyond Earth.

Section 4: Three Perspectives United

Rick Stroud's *The Book of the Moon* offers a clear, evidence-based overview of the Moon, blending scientific insight with historical and cultural perspectives. He explains accepted theories like the Giant Impact Hypothesis and explores data from Apollo missions to illuminate the Moon's structure and behavior. Stroud's approach is informative and grounded, aiming to deepen understanding of the Moon through both scientific detail and humanity's long-standing fascination with it.

In *Who Built the Moon?*, Christopher Knight and Alan Butler put forth a speculative hypothesis that the Moon is an artificial construct, deliberately engineered to support life on Earth. They argue that the Moon's size, orbit, and mathematical relationships to Earth and the Sun are too precise to be coincidental. Drawing from ancient measurement systems, lunar anomalies, and solar eclipse symmetry, they suggest intelligent design—possibly by extraterrestrials or future humans—and introduce metaphysical ideas such as time loops and the Möbius Principle to propose that life on Earth may have required the Moon's engineered presence.

A.J. Gentile expands on lunar anomalies by pointing to geological and chemical irregularities that challenge mainstream lunar formation theories. He highlights inverted stratigraphy, hollow-like internal structures, rare high-strength metals, radioactive isotopes, and magnetic remnants that seem inconsistent with natural processes. Gentile references ancient cultural accounts of a Moonless Earth and aligns lunar phenomena with catastrophic Earth events like the Younger Dryas, suggesting that the Moon's presence—possibly artificial—may be tied to pivotal moments in Earth's history, even predating our own planet.

Together, these three perspectives form a layered and multidimensional view of the Moon. Stroud offers a grounded, factual foundation; Knight and Butler challenge the boundaries of mainstream thought by exploring mathematical coincidences and intelligent design; Gentile connects physical anomalies to historical disruptions and cultural memory. Despite differing in tone and credibility, all three perspectives converge on a central idea: the Moon, far from being a simple rock in the sky, may hold deeper mysteries—scientific, existential, and possibly even intentional—that invite both critical inquiry and imaginative exploration.

Section 5: Moon's Role in Earth's Stability

The Moon plays a vital role in stabilizing Earth's axial tilt, which currently sits at about 23.5 degrees—a tilt that gives us our four seasons. Without the Moon's steady gravitational pull, Earth's axis would wobble wildly over time, triggering dramatic and unpredictable climate shifts. Such instability would make it far more difficult for complex life—like humans—to evolve or survive.[341]

The Moon also exerts a powerful tidal influence that has gradually slowed Earth's rotation. Without it, our planet might spin much faster, with days lasting only 6 to 8 hours and rotational speeds reaching 3,000 to 4,000 miles per hour—conditions that would be extreme, violent, and likely catastrophic for life. Instead, thanks to the Moon, Earth rotates at a gentler pace of about 1,000 miles per hour, giving us 24-hour days.[342]

The Moon is not just a distant satellite—it is a key ingredient in the recipe for life on Earth. Its presence seems less like a cosmic accident and more like an element of precise natural design.

Section 6: Moon's Two-Faced Nature Revisited

The Moon is not only essential for Earth's stability and the conditions that support life, but it also displays several unusual and intriguing characteristics.

As previously mentioned, several times, the Moon is unusually large relative to Earth and perfectly positioned—400 times smaller than the Sun yet 400 times closer—allowing for the rare and precise alignment of total solar eclipses. Its rotation is synchronized with Earth's, always showing the same face.

The near side of the Moon looks dramatically different from the far side: the near side is smoother and darker, dominated by vast basalt plains known as maria, while the far side is brighter, more rugged, and densely cratered. These visual differences reflect a structural asymmetry: the Moon's crust is significantly thinner on the near side, at approximately 25 miles, whereas the far-side crust measures about 37 miles—a difference of roughly 12 miles.

The Moon appears nearly spherical and even hollow in structure, with oddly uniform crater depths. Its surface dust contains unexpected concentrations of metals typically associated with nuclear byproducts.

Section 7: Closing Reflection

The Moon refuses to be reduced to a single explanation. Through *The Book of the Moon*, *Who Built the Moon?*, and *The Why Files*, we see how one celestial body can inspire disciplined science, bold speculation, and ongoing debate. It stabilizes Earth and makes life possible, yet it also provokes questions about coincidence, design, and cosmic purpose.

Whether understood as natural satellite or profound mystery, the Moon remains both scientifically essential and philosophically unsettling—familiar in the sky, yet never fully explained.

CHAPTER 5
Anomalous Structures on the Moon

Claims persist that extraterrestrial bases exist on the far side of the Moon. Several witnesses cited in Dr. Steven Greer's *Unacknowledged* and A.J. Gentile's *The Why Files:* "The Dark Side of the Moon" report having seen photographs or documents allegedly depicting artificial structures or installations not attributable to human activity.

These supposed lunar bases are said to be known by select factions within the government but deliberately concealed from the public—mirroring the broader secrecy surrounding the extraterrestrial phenomenon. Some witnesses further allege that NASA or other space agencies have intentionally suppressed this information by altering photographic evidence or classifying relevant materials.

Section 1: Orbiter Missions and Anomalous Structures

Prior to the Apollo Moon landings, the Soviet Union achieved a historic milestone in 1959 when its Luna 3 orbiter became the first spacecraft to photograph the far side of the Moon, revealing a landscape strikingly different from the familiar near side.

Years later, in preparation for Apollo, NASA's five Lunar Orbiter flyover missions from August 1966 to August 1967 went on to capture approximately 99% of the Moon's surface in high detail. Together, these missions produced the first comprehensive images of the far side, which appeared to show ancient, pristine structures—believed by some to be the work of advanced extraterrestrial beings.[343]

Section 2: Isolation on the Far Side of the Moon

What's all the hype around the Artemis II mission—a crewed flight set to orbit the Moon again in April 2026—when humans already accomplished this nearly 60 years ago?

The first crewed mission to orbit the Moon—completing ten orbits, including passes over its far side—was Apollo 8 in December 1968. During each pass behind the Moon, the astronauts lost communication with Earth for about 45 minutes. Frank Borman, James Lovell, and William Anders systematically photographed the Moon's surface, including its far side. They made history as the first humans to leave Earth's orbit, travel to the Moon, orbit it, capture images of the far side, and return safely.

In July 1969, during the Apollo 11 mission, while Neil Armstrong and Buzz Aldrin explored the Moon's near side, their colleague Michael Collins remained alone in the Command Module, orbiting at an altitude of about 60 miles. Collins became the most isolated human in history, losing all radio contact with Earth for approximately 45 minutes during each pass behind the Moon. During that portion of every orbit, he was completely cut off from communication—a profound solitude no human had ever experienced before.[344] In his flight journal, Collins wrote:

> I am alone now, truly alone, and absolutely isolated from any known life. I am it. If a count were taken, the score would be three billion plus two on the other side of the Moon, and one plus God knows what on this side.[345]

Though poetic, his words hinted at an unsettling awareness. During earlier missions, astronauts had already begun to report strange phenomena from the Moon's far side.[346]

During the moonwalk on the near side of the Moon, Armstrong and Aldrin planted the American flag, collected samples, and left behind symbolic items—including a gold olive branch representing peace and a silicon disc, the size of a half-dollar coin, inscribed with microscopic messages of goodwill from 73 world leaders.[347] Why bring messages of peace to a supposedly empty world? It is because the Apollo 11 crew was warned that when they landed on the Moon, they wouldn't be alone.[348]

Section 3: "Missing Minutes" and Alleged Transcripts

Some researchers argue that not everything that happened during the mission was revealed. There are persistent rumors about a "missing" two-minute segment of radio communication between the astronauts and Mission Control—two minutes that were, according to some, censored or redacted from public release.[349]

Transcripts allegedly describe Neil Armstrong observing "structures" arranged in a geometric pattern at the edge of a nearby crater. In one transmission, he reportedly says: "There are other spaceships. They're lined up on the other side of the crater there. There they are, and they're watching us. And it's obvious they don't want us to be here."[350]

NASA has consistently denied the existence of these transcripts, attributing the so-called "missing minutes" to technical issues or fabrication. Still, many believe Armstrong and Aldrin may have encountered something unexpected—something never meant to reach the public.[351]

Section 4: Apollo 11 Press Conference Anomaly

After returning from the Moon, the Apollo 11 crew appeared before the press. But instead of jubilant heroes, the world saw three emotionally distant, somber men.[352] Their demeanor was striking: eyes downcast, shoulders slouched, voices subdued—almost as if they were depressed.

What should have been a historic celebration instead felt like a somber debriefing.[353]

Neil Armstrong, typically confident and articulate, spoke haltingly. Buzz Aldrin looked dazed, as if burdened by something he couldn't say. Michael Collins maintained composure, but his tone was measured and carefully restrained.[354]

Why did the three men who had just completed humanity's most awe-inspiring technological achievement appear so emotionally detached—almost disturbed?[355] It is highly likely that the astronauts witnessed something on the Moon they were ordered not to reveal. Some suggest they were warned, debriefed, or even threatened before the press conference to ensure total silence.[356]

Section 5: Apollo 14 and Edgar Mitchell's Claims

When Edgar Mitchell piloted the Apollo 14 lunar module to a landing near the rim of Cone Crater in February 1971, the mission aimed to collect subsurface material. However, he and Alan Shepard stopped short of the crater's edge because the area was occupied by extraterrestrial vehicles (ETVs).[357]

In 2013, Mitchell participated in the National Press Club in Washington, D.C., via Skype, from April 29th to May 3rd. In his own words, Mitchell supports his claim of having seen aliens on the Moon:

> We have been visited by alien visitors from different star systems and different civilizations.... We are not alone in the universe. They have been coming here for a very long time. The evidence suggests that we have been receiving visitors for perhaps hundreds, maybe even thousands, of years.[358]

Edgar Mitchell asserts that extraterrestrials have visited Earth for centuries, reflecting his personal belief that humanity is not alone in the universe despite a lack of verified scientific evidence supporting the claim.

Section 6: Warnings and Continued Astronaut Silence

The astronauts have remained silent about the Moon bases and the presence of extraterrestrials after being warned that revealing the truth could cost not only their own lives but also the lives of their families. Neil Armstrong has claimed that humanity was, in fact, warned off the Moon.[359]

Section 7: Whistleblowers and Insider Testimonies

Over the decades, numerous individuals with alleged ties to NASA, the military, and defense contractors have come forward, claiming direct knowledge of alien structures or activity on the Moon. Their stories—often dismissed by officials—have nonetheless left a lasting impact on public curiosity.[360]

Section 8: Wolfe and the Lunar Orbiter Photographs

In 1965, Karl Wolfe, a U.S. Air Force precision electronics technician with top-secret clearance, was assigned to assist the Lunar Orbiter Project at Langley Air Force Base, alongside international personnel and technicians from other countries.

One day, while repairing photographic equipment in a classified darkroom, he struck up a conversation with another technician who casually stated: "By the way, we've discovered a base on the back side of the Moon."[361] The technician then showed him a series of high-resolution images—photos that appeared to show artificial structures on the Moon. According to Wolfe, some structures looked like "cooling towers at generating power plants," others were "very straight and tall with a flat top," some were "round," and one resembled "a Quonset hut, with a dome, like a greenhouse."[362]

In 2001, Wolfe participated in a national press conference organized by the *Disclosure Project.* There, he publicly stated: "I will testify under oath before Congress that what I'm saying is the truth." Shortly after this disclosure, Wolfe died in a mysterious bicycle accident—struck by a truck under circumstances some researchers consider suspicious.[363]

Section 9: Johnston and the Suppressed Evidence

Dr. Ken Johnston, a former manager at NASA's Lunar Receiving Laboratory during the Apollo program, has alleged that he personally handled photographic and video evidence showing ruins, domed cities, and gravity-defying machinery on the Moon. Johnston says he was ordered to destroy these photos and films—but instead, he secretly kept copies. In 1995, he went public, asserting that NASA was hiding evidence of extraterrestrial activity. Not long after, he was terminated and never again allowed to work with NASA.[364]

Section 10: Hare and the Airbrushed UFOs

From 1970 to 1971, Donna Hare worked at NASA as a contractor with secret clearance in Building 8 at the Johnson Space Center, where high-resolution space photographs were routinely processed. She later recounted an encounter with a technician who claimed to have seen original photographs showing a craft hovering above the lunar surface—images that, according to him, were quickly altered or suppressed.[365]

Hare explained that in NASA's film lab a technician once showed her aerial shots of the lunar surface. Pointing to an unusual object, she asked, "Is this a UFO?" The technician replied, "I can't tell you that." When she asked what they did with such information, he told her, "We always have to airbrush them out before we release them to the public."[366] Hare expressed surprise that there appeared to be an established protocol for removing UFO images from NASA photographs.[367]

She also recalled that some individuals later warned her not to discuss the subject. Although they did not directly threaten her, Hare said the experience left her feeling that "this topic was like sex—you know, everybody knew about it, but nobody talked about it in mixed company."[368]

She further claimed that the technician who had shown her the photos was later relocated by NASA and, according to her, "disappeared off the face of the Earth."[369] Hare states that a man she knew well—who had been in "quarantine with the astronauts"—told her that ET craft were present on the Moon during the Apollo 11 landing, and that he later "disappeared off the face of the Earth."[370]

In 2001, Hare testified during the *Disclosure Project,* repeating her claims about the airbrushing of UFO evidence from Moon photos. She stated that employees were instructed to "airbrush" anomalies—unexplained objects—out of images before they were publicly released.[371]

Section 11: Dean and the Destroyed Apollo Film

U.S. Army Command Sergeant Major Robert Dean, who held NATO Cosmic Top Secret clearance, claimed that NASA destroyed 40 rolls of Apollo mission film. According to Dean, the films contained undeniable images of enormous alien craft, massive buildings, and ancient structures—particularly around the Lansberg Crater. He stated that astronauts were specifically ordered to photograph this region during multiple missions. However, he alleged that these photos were never released to the public.[372]

Section 12: Arms Race and Cancelation of Apollo Missions

According to some interpretations, humanity was warned off the Moon because lunar activity became entangled in the Cold War arms race.[373] Instead of seeking peaceful exploration, our intentions were driven by greed—an attempt to seize extraterrestrial technology and energy resources for personal gain, rather than fostering genuine peace and understanding.[374] After a few more lunar landings—and growing signs of extraterrestrial presence—the Apollo missions were abruptly canceled, only to be replaced by the Shuttle program.[375]

Section 13: Implications of Extraterrestrial Presence

If there are alien bases, artificial structures, or ancient ruins on the Moon the implications are staggering. It would mean we are not alone, and we never were. It could explain the secrecy, the lost footage, the canceled missions, and the strange behavior of astronauts.

But it also raises troubling questions: If someone—or something—has been watching the Moon all along, what will happen when we return? Are we being permitted to explore again, or are we trespassing on territory that was never ours to claim?

The idea that an unknown intelligence has been continuously observing or monitoring the Moon over time implies a speculative fear that humans may not be alone in space and that returning to the Moon could mean entering territory already claimed or overseen by someone or something else.

Section 14: Closing Reflection

If there are extraterrestrials on the Moon, it seems they have made it clear that humanity's path to becoming an interplanetary civilization depends on four key principles articulated by Dr. Steven Greer: being civilized, living in peace, renouncing weapons of mass destruction, and venturing into space without weaponry, guided by a consciousness of universal peace.[376] A poem echoes this vision:

> From the silent depths of the cosmos, extraterrestrials came—guardians of a dying world, standing between Earth and the insatiable virus of humankind's greed, which would trade peace for profit and turn the planet to ash.[377]

CHAPTER 6
Voyager 1

Launched by NASA in 1977, Voyager 1 is heading toward the constellation Ophiuchus, specifically in the direction of a faint red dwarf star known as Gliese 445, located approximately 17.6 light-years away in the Milky Way Galaxy.[378, 379] Since Gliese 445 is moving toward our Solar System and Voyager 1 travels at 10.5 miles per second, the spacecraft will take nearly 41,600 years to reach its closest approach to this star.[380]

Section 1: The Serpent Bearer and Gliese 445

The constellation Ophiuchus, known as the Serpent Bearer, is a large and significant region of the sky, rich in stellar, nebular, and galactic phenomena, and it contains Gliese 445. Located along the celestial equator and intersecting the plane of the Milky Way, Ophiuchus offers astronomers a fascinating field filled with dark nebulae, star clusters, and notable stars. As Voyager 1 travels toward Gliese 445, its voyage evokes a fitting symbolic journey into a constellation so full of cosmic variety.[381, 382]

Section 2: Endurance Beyond Technology

One of the most astonishing aspects of Voyager 1 is how primitive its technology is by today's standards—and yet it continues to function, over 48 years after launch.[383] Voyager 1 contains three onboard computers, each responsible for different systems: command, attitude control, and science data. The total memory of these systems is about 68 kilobytes combined—less than a single JPEG image. By comparison, a modern smartphone contains several gigabytes of RAM, hundreds of gigabytes to terabytes of storage, and CPUs millions of times faster than Voyager's hardware.[384]

The spacecraft transmits data using a 20-watt radio transmitter, about the power of a refrigerator lightbulb. Even so, the Deep Space Network on Earth can still detect its faint signal from over 15 billion miles away. Data rates are extremely slow—about 160 bits per second, not kilobits.[385]

Voyager 1 is powered by radioisotope thermoelectric generators (RTGs) that convert heat from decaying plutonium-238 into electricity. Its original output was about 470 watts but has degraded to less than 250 watts, forcing engineers to shut down instruments over time to preserve basic operations.[386]

Section 3: The Golden Record

Though the spacecraft's mission is expected to last millions of years—far outliving humanity—it carries a "Golden Record" containing 115 images, natural sounds, and greetings in fifty-five languages for any potential extraterrestrial civilizations that may one day encounter it.[387, 388]

Despite its outdated technology, Voyager 1 remains one of humanity's greatest engineering achievements—not because of its computing power, but because it was built to last, and to travel farther than anything before or since.[389]

Section 4: Ophiuchus' Stellar Neighborhood

Among the notable stars in Ophiuchus is Rasalhague (Alpha Ophiuchi), the brightest star in the constellation. It is a bluish-white giant located about 48 light-years from Earth.[390] Another significant star is Barnard's Star, located just 6 light-years from our solar system, making it one of the nearest stellar neighbors. This red dwarf is about 48% cooler than the Sun and exhibits the fastest apparent motion across Earth's sky. It has also drawn significant interest as a candidate for hosting potential planetary systems.[391]

Ophiuchus is home to several intriguing nebulae, particularly dark nebulae—dense clouds of gas and dust that block background starlight. Among them is Barnard 68, a small but famous dark nebula that appears as a black void in the starry background. This object is part of the larger Ophiuchus Molecular Cloud, a nearby star-forming region located about 460 light-years from Earth.[392]

Another notable dark nebula partly located in Ophiuchus is the Pipe Nebula, a large complex of cold gas that contributes to the silhouette of the "Dark Horse Nebula" visible near the galactic bulge. These regions are critical for studying the earliest stages of stellar formation.[393]

Ophiuchus contains both globular and open star clusters, each offering a different glimpse into the life cycles of stars. Among the most prominent globular clusters are Messier 10 (M10), Messier 12 (M12), Messier 14 (M14), and Messier 107 (M107). These are dense, spherical collections of tens to hundreds of thousands of old stars. They orbit the Milky Way's core and are some of the oldest structures in the galaxy. Observing them gives astronomers insight into the early universe.[394]

In contrast, IC 4665 is a young open star cluster of a few hundred to a few thousand stars, located about 1,100 light-years away. It's 33 light-years across and about 30 to 40 million years old—very young in cosmic terms. Its stars are mostly blue and hot, as they are still young and burning brightly, making the cluster an excellent example of early stellar evolution. IC 4665 lies in one of the Milky Way's spiral arms, situated in the outer region of the galaxy's disk.[395]

Although Ophiuchus lies along the plane of the Milky Way, the Ophiuchus Supercluster—including the Ophiuchus Galaxy Cluster at its center—is far beyond our galaxy, located about 390 million light-years from Earth. Its central galaxy, NeVe 1, experienced a massive energetic outburst in 2020, likely powered by a supermassive black hole that consumed an estimated 270 million solar masses of material—highlighting the extraordinary scale of energy involved.[396]

One of the most iconic moments in Voyager 1's journey occurred in February 1990, when the spacecraft turned its camera back toward Earth beyond the planet Pluto and captured a photograph of our planet from a distance of 3.7 billion miles. This image, known as the "Pale Blue Dot," shows Earth as a tiny speck of light in the vastness of space—just about 1/1,000th of a pixel in size.[397] The photograph serves as a humbling reminder of our place in the universe and has become an enduring symbol of humanity's fragility and resilience.

Yet, despite this humbling view, humanity's history is marked by pain and conflict. We have inflicted suffering on our own species through territorial wars, torture, discrimination, and systemic violence—whether physical, political, or psychological, such as bullying and hate speech. Tragically, this cycle of harm continues today in various forms, including genocidal conflicts and the threat of nuclear annihilation. As inhabitants of this fragile pale blue dot, we face a crucial choice: to rise above our divisions and protect this unique world, or risk destroying the very home that other possible life forms might one day see from afar.

In 2012, Voyager 1 became the first human-made object to enter interstellar space—the region beyond the Sun's protective bubble where space is filled with gas and dust between the stars.[398] As of February 2026, Voyager 1 is approximately 15.8 billion miles from Earth and is expected to reach one light-day in distance, roughly 16 billion miles, by November 2026. A signal from Earth now takes 23 hours 30 minutes or more to reach it. Despite dwindling power from its radioisotope thermoelectric generator (RTG), Voyager 1 continues to send back data, offering rare insights into the outer reaches of the galaxy.[399]

Section 6: *Star Trek—The Motion Picture*

The themes of space exploration and human potential in *Star Trek: The Motion Picture* (1979) resonate with real-world scientific achievements, particularly the Voyager missions.

Set in 2273, the film reunites the original USS Enterprise crew and centers on V'Ger, a mysterious alien entity revealed to be Voyager 6, a fictional human spacecraft launched in the 20th-century transformed by an advanced alien race.[400] Returning to Earth as a super-intelligent being seeking its creator, V'Ger mirrors humanity's fascination with exploration and the potential for our creations to surpass us.[401]

The narrative draws heavily on the real Voyager 1, launched in 1977 and completing its Jupiter flyby in March 1979 while still transmitting data as the film premiered in December 1979.[402] Like V'Ger, Voyager 1 symbolizes the drive to explore the unknown, having gathered invaluable data about the gas giants before continuing into deep space.[403]

By situating V'Ger's story roughly 200 years after Voyager 1's launch, the film reflects both optimism and anxiety about the future—advanced technology, interstellar travel, and communication with sentient machines.[404]

CHAPTER 7
The Alien Question

The Aboriginal peoples of Australia possess one of the world's oldest continuous cultures, with traditions and knowledge spanning over 60,000 years—far older than Stonehenge in England or even the pyramids of Egypt.[405] Aboriginal elder Kevin Gavi Duncan emphasizes this longevity, stating, "Our stories are 20,000 to 30,000 years older than the pyramids of Egypt."[406]

Section 1: Aboriginal Myths of Star Visitors

This deep cultural heritage is vividly expressed through ancient Aboriginal cave art, which preserves profound cosmological stories of beings from the stars—visitors who once interacted with humanity. A notable example is the Wandjina figures from the northwest Kimberley region, featuring large white faces, black oval eyes, and halo-like shapes.[407] These images strikingly resemble modern depictions of "grey aliens," prompting ancient astronaut theorists to interpret them as representations of extraterrestrial visitors.[408]

Aboriginal elder Gary Simon Jagamarra highlights the importance of this art in preserving memory: "We carved them, we sang them, we danced them in stories, we painted them—so when the visitors left, we didn't forget about them."[409] Through cave art and oral tradition, sacred knowledge and cosmic events remain alive across generations, connecting the past to the present.

Interestingly, Australia continues to be a focal point for UFO phenomena today. Modern investigations have identified it as a hotspot for UFO activity, particularly in the Blue Mountains. In 2015, filmmaker Damien Nott released a collection of over 2,000 UFO images captured across the Australian skies within just three years. Nott described the sightings as "morphing in shape and rotating," a phenomenon that has drawn growing public interest.[410]

This ongoing fascination with the skies echoes in Australia's iconic landscapes, such as Uluru. Also known as Ayers Rock, this massive sandstone monolith in Australia's Northern Territory is estimated to be 550 million years old.[411] It rises over 1,100 feet and spans a circumference of six miles. Geologists believe it is the visible tip of a vast underground rock formation. According to local lore, Uluru has a cosmic origin—formed when a celestial spear from the Pleiades star cluster struck Earth, seeding humanity.[412] This story aligns with the ancient astronaut theory, which suggests extraterrestrial influence on early human life.

Additional clues to ancient contact appear in the Gosford Glyphs found in Brisbane Water National Park, New South Wales. These two eight-foot-high rock walls have over 300 carvings that resemble Egyptian hieroglyphs rather than traditional Aboriginal art.[413] Egyptologist Ray Johnson deciphered the inscriptions and concluded they describe the burial of Lord Nefer-ti-ru, an Egyptian royal who died in Australia between 2637 and 2614 BCE while visiting with his brother.[414] The glyphs reportedly mark his final resting place.

When the site was visited by a couple of researchers, they observed panels depicting a UFO-shaped symbol and a story about two Egyptian princes shipwrecked in Australia—one of whom was bitten by a snake and buried there.[415] Johnson's translations were reviewed by Egyptian scholars, including Dr. Abou Dia' Ghazi of the Cairo Library, who agreed that the script resembled a "proto-Egyptian" writing system dating back around 4,600 years.[416]

Together, these threads of ancient wisdom preserved by the Aboriginal peoples may offer profound insights into humanity's cosmic origins and future. As modern science continues to explore the universe and consciousness, the teachings of Australia's oldest living culture remind us that humanity's connection to the stars is a long-established truth.

Section 2: Erich von Däniken—*Chariots of the Gods*

On July 20, 1969, Neil Armstrong and Buzz Aldrin became the first humans to land on the Moon, sparking widespread curiosity about extraterrestrial life and whether aliens had visited Earth in ancient times.[417]

Erich von Däniken's 1968 book *Chariots of the Gods* argues that extraterrestrial visitors influenced ancient civilizations. In 2008, the Vatican acknowledged that belief in extraterrestrials didn't conflict with faith in God, opening the door to new interpretations of humanity's place in the universe.[418]

In his book, von Däniken observes an incident the prophet Ezekiel experienced approximately 2,600 years ago.[419] Ezekiel described a vivid vision of a fiery chariot emerging from the clouds—a windstorm of flashing lightning and glowing skies, accompanied by four living beings and strange, interlocking wheels:

> I looked up and saw a windstorm coming from the north. Lightning was flashing from a huge cloud, and the sky around it was glowing... I saw what looked like four living creatures in human form... As I was looking... I saw four wheels... Each had another wheel intersecting it... The rims... were covered with eyes... Whenever the creatures moved, the wheels moved with them...[420]

Von Däniken argues that this is not a mystical vision but a detailed account of an alien spacecraft. He points out that Ezekiel never uses the word "God" in the original Hebrew; instead, he refers to the fiery chariot or vehicle he is seeing as the "Splendor of the Highest."[421] When the Splendor of the Highest descends, it produces a sound like the roar of a waterfall. Atop it, Ezekiel sees something like a capsule, and within it something resembling a throne; seated on the throne is a figure with the appearance of a human.[422]

Theologian Barry Downing supports this view, suggesting ancient people described advanced technology in spiritual terms due to a lack of understanding.[423] NASA engineer Josef Blumrich was influenced by this interpretation that he used Ezekiel's descriptions to help model the landing gear for NASA's Mariner Mars mission.[424]

Ezekiel also recounts being "lifted by a spirit," describing experiences akin to modern abduction narratives—being shown structures, given a mission, then returned.[425] Although he lacked the vocabulary for a "spaceship," von Däniken observes that Ezekiel recorded what he witnessed as faithfully as possible using the language available to him at the time.[426]

While some point to sacred texts as possible records of extraordinary encounters, others turn to physical landscapes for evidence they believe may suggest similar phenomena.

Section 3: The Nazca Lines

Stretching across the dry plains of southern Peru, the Nazca Lines are among the world's most mysterious ancient creations. Etched over 2,000 years ago, they include miles-long straight lines, geometric shapes, and massive figures of animals like monkeys, birds, and spiders—some over 1,000 feet long.[427] One of the most unusual is the so-called "Astronaut," a humanoid figure with a large head and raised arm, seemingly waving to the sky.[428]

Some ancient astronaut theorists have suggested that the Nazca Lines were made as landing sites for extraterrestrial spacecraft, pointing to the vast, runway-like shapes and their visibility from above.[429] While mainstream archaeology sees them as religious or astronomical symbols, the ancient astronaut theory interprets them as messages or markers for celestial visitors.[430]

Unlike the Nazca Lines carved into the ground, the Serpent Mound in Ohio was built up from the earth itself, yet both structures provoke similar questions about ancient knowledge, celestial symbolism, and the possibility of otherworldly connections.[431]

Section 4: Artifacts, Ancient Tech, Reliefs, Megaliths

Across cultures and continents, ancient texts and artifacts hint at knowledge and technologies that challenge conventional historical narratives. In India, epics like the *Mahabharata, Rigveda,* and *Ramayana* describe vimanas—flying machines capable of emitting destructive beams and appearing in multiple places at once.[432] The *Bhagavata Purana* even depicts kings piloting metal aircraft.[433] Researcher Michael Cremo suggests that these accounts, some over 5,000 years old, may reflect eyewitness reports of real technology rather than pure mythology.[434] Giorgio Tsoukalos, researcher and host of the *Ancient Aliens* documentary series, observes that belief in celestial vehicles and divine visitors remains deeply ingrained in Indian culture and uncontroversial.[435]

Similarly, in Colombia, archaeologists have uncovered thousands of small gold artifacts resembling airplanes discovered in ancient tombs.[436] Objects—such as wings, fuselages, and tail fins—along with astronaut-like sculptures, suggest knowledge of aeronautical design far beyond what is typically attributed to pre-Columbian civilizations, possibly indicating ancient contact with extraterrestrial beings.[437]

At the Mayan site of Palenque, the sarcophagus of King Pakal—who ruled for 68 years in the 7th century—remained hidden for over a thousand years, sealed beneath an incredibly heavy lid. The sarcophagus lid depicts Pakal reclining in a cocoon-like seat within a capsule-like object, manipulating what appears to be a set of controls with one hand while seemingly adjusting a device with the other. The heel of his left foot rests on what resembles a pedal. He wears what appears to be a face mask, with an apparatus extending from his mouth, and affixed to his chest is some form of monitoring device. Flames erupt from what looks like an engine beneath the capsule.[438, 439] Jason Martell, a leading researcher in ancient civilizations, has noted the carving's uncanny resemblance to modern depictions of astronauts in spaceflight, suggesting that the Maya may have been illustrating encounters with advanced beings.[440]

Beyond airborne technology, other ancient artifacts hint at sophisticated, sometimes enigmatic, technologies. The Antikythera mechanism of Greece functioned as a complex mechanical computer, while the Baghdad Battery may have generated electricity.[441] Carvings at Egypt's Temple of Dendera resemble light bulbs, raising questions about how ancient chambers were illuminated without soot or torches.[442] While mainstream explanations—such as symbolic imagery, mirrors, or electroplating—exist, some theorists argue these point to lost technologies.[443]

Megalithic construction adds another layer of mystery. From Egypt to Mesoamerica, India, and remote Pacific islands, massive stone structures exhibit remarkable precision. The global recurrence of pyramids and other monuments has led theorists like von Däniken and Tsoukalos to suggest that these feats may reflect shared advanced knowledge or contact with beings described in myths as "gods from the sky." Skeptics, meanwhile, attribute these achievements to exceptional human ingenuity and astronomical skill.

Whether interpreted as evidence of extraterrestrial visitation, forgotten technologies, or extraordinary human creativity, these artifacts and legends continue to challenge our understanding of the ancient world—and invite us to reconsider the origins of civilization.

Section 5: What Lies Beneath Antarctica's Ice?

Antarctica is a vast continent larger than the mainland United States and even greater in area than Europe. It hides enormous natural resources, including hundreds of billions of barrels of oil, though the Antarctic Treaty prevents any extraction and keeps the continent dedicated to peaceful scientific research.[444] Seven nations once claimed portions of Antarctica, but these claims are now frozen under the treaty.

Antarctica is the least explored and most mysterious continent due to its extreme cold, violent winds, and the incredible thickness of its ice—averaging about 1.2 miles and reaching depths of 3 miles, or roughly five to six times taller than the Burj Khalifa, the tallest building in the world.[445] Beneath this ice, Antarctica would not appear as a single landmass but rather a collection of rugged islands, mountains, and deep basins that have been unified only by the weight of the ice sheet.[446]

Antarctica was once part of the supercontinent Gondwana and was connected to Africa and South America before tectonic forces separated them. When the Drake Passage opened about 35 million years ago, a circumpolar current formed, isolating Antarctica and allowing the massive ice sheet to develop.[447] Beneath the ice, scientists have also discovered what may be one of the largest asteroid-impact structures on Earth: the Wilkes Land crater, a massive and still-debated formation that suggests a colossal impact event in the distant past.[448]

Despite the harsh conditions, scientists have found life buried beneath about 2,600 feet of Antarctic ice. In subglacial Lake Whillans, isolated for millions of years, researchers discovered living microorganisms, proving that life can exist even in extreme, dark, and isolated environments—offering clues to where life may exist beyond Earth.[449]

The mystery deepens with Antarctica. Some believe that hidden beneath its ice lies the oldest pyramid on Earth—possibly the prototype for all others. Antarctica, a vast and largely unexplored continent spanning over five million square miles, remains shrouded in ice up to three miles thick. For millions of years, it has been considered uninhabited, yet in recent decades, photographs and satellite imagery have revealed pyramid-like formations emerging from melting ice.[450]

In 1929, historians discovered a map painted on gazelle hide that defied conventional understanding. Known as the Piri Reis map, it was created by Piri Reis, a 16th-century Ottoman admiral and cartographer.[451]

What made the map extraordinary was that it depicted the coasts of Europe and North Africa that had not yet been explored at the time, including the ice-free coastline of Antarctica.[452]

The map shows Antarctica's shoreline not as it appears beneath miles of ice today, but as it would have looked when the continent was ice-free—millions of years ago.[453] The map's precision has led to persistent speculation: Did ancient civilizations possess advanced knowledge? Or could extraterrestrial intelligence have played a role? Such questions fuel continuing debate about what secrets remain beneath Antarctica's ice.

Section 6: Global Links of the Great Pyramid

These discoveries tie into broader ancient astronaut theories, which question how ancient civilizations were able to construct massive monuments with such remarkable engineering precision.

The Great Pyramid of Giza, built from more than 2.5 million limestone and granite blocks weighing several tons each, is believed by mainstream archaeologists to have been completed in just 22 years, around 2560 BCE.[454] Alternative archaeologists, however, date its construction much earlier—to about 10,500 BCE.

Tsoukalos argues that completing such a structure in just 22 years would require setting a block "every nine seconds," a pace he claims would be impossible even with modern technology.[455] The pyramid's design adds to its mystery: when viewed from above, it becomes clear that it does not have four flat sides but eight, due to the subtle concavity on each face that creates a slight inward slope.

Many of the stones used in the pyramid's construction are enormous and were fitted together with astounding precision. Inside the Grand Gallery, for instance, there are two adjacent stones whose grain patterns flow seamlessly from one to the other, with no material loss in between.[456] How could this have been achieved? It appears to defy explanation. Using crude tools such as chisels, hammers, or thick blades, he notes, it would be nearly impossible to replicate such flawless joints without any material being chipped away.[457]

The mysteries don't end there. How were these enormous stones—each weighing an average of two and a half tons, with some estimated at "50 to 80 tons"—transported, and from where?"[458] Even more perplexing is how they were lifted and set in place without the use of wheels or pulleys, which, according to mainstream Egyptologists, had not yet been invented at the time.[459]

There is little doubt that the Great Pyramid was built by the ancient Egyptians. However, some ancient Egyptian texts suggest they did not work alone. These texts speak of assistance from beings referred to as the "Guardians of the Sky"—which ancient astronaut theorists interpret as extraterrestrial beings.[460]

Tsoukalos points out that our ancestors lacked the vocabulary to describe modern technologies such as engines, cranes, machines, motors, helicopter blades, or fuel pumps. Instead, they described what they witnessed using the language available to them, drawing on familiar concepts to express extraordinary experiences.[461]

Tsoukalos makes an intriguing observation: there is no clear technological progression leading up to the construction of the pyramids.[462] By contrast, when we examine the evolution of the automobile—from the Ford Model T to the Ford Taurus—we can trace a steady line of development. With the pyramids, however, no such evolution is evident.[463] The ancient Egyptians managed to work with massive monolithic blocks, some weighing over 500 tons—a feat unmatched even today using standard building materials, which are typically brick-sized in comparison.[464]

Tsoukalos observes that pyramids are not unique to Egypt—they appear across the world. Stepped pyramids exist in Central America, ziggurats in ancient Sumer, and similar structures in China, Greece, and Indonesia.[465] He says, "Ecuador is filled with pyramids inside the jungle that have remained unexplored."[466] Tsoukalos remarks that the Great Pyramid of Cholula in Mexico is the world's largest monument by volume, with a mass of 4.45 million cubic meters—nearly double that of Egypt's Great Pyramid, which contains about 2.5 million cubic meters.[467] The global presence of such structures, he suggests, points to the influence—or perhaps the direct intervention—of the same extraterrestrial beings.[468]

Pyramids around the world—from Egypt and Peru to China, Bosnia, and Indonesia—share striking architectural, astronomical, and mathematical similarities, suggesting either exceptional human ingenuity or guidance from advanced knowledge, possibly extraterrestrial.[469] The Great Pyramid of Giza, precisely aligned with stars and magnetic north, along with structures like Teotihuacan and Borobudur, hints at cosmic or spiritual purposes beyond tombs or temples.

Theories propose that pyramids functioned as energy devices, harnessing Earth's electromagnetic fields.[470] Experiments suggest they can influence biological and physical matter, implying ancient civilizations may have intentionally located them at geophysically potent sites.[471] Hidden, submerged, or off-limits pyramids in Alaska, Antarctica, Japan, and China add to speculation of a lost global civilization with advanced knowledge, preserved across continents.[472]

Some theorists connect these monuments to a planetary energy grid, potentially used for wireless power, navigation, or communication, possibly influenced by extraterrestrial visitors.[473] Historical accounts—from Antarctic expeditions to ancient myths—hint at forgotten civilizations and technologies, including advanced energy systems like those suggested by the Baghdad Battery or Dendera reliefs.[474]

Overall, pyramids may represent more than monuments: they could be evidence of a global network of energy, knowledge, and cosmic connection, challenging conventional understanding of human history and hinting at a lost link between humanity and advanced technology.

Section 7: Marine Fossils in Egyptian Pyramids

In 2008, researchers from the University of the Aegean and the University of Athens analyzed the limestone blocks used to construct Egypt's monuments and discovered that they contained vast quantities of marine fossils.[475] The finding reignited debate over whether the pyramid stones were carved from natural quarries or cast like ancient concrete.[476] For ancient astronaut theorists, however, this discovery raised an entirely different question: could the pyramids themselves have once been underwater?

Fossil evidence indicates that the region may have been submerged in the distant past.[477] To some, this points toward a global cataclysm—perhaps the very flood described in ancient texts termed the Younger Dryas. Many traditions, including the Biblical account of the flood, describe a deluge sent to cleanse or reset humanity. But what if, as some theorists suggest, this flood was not divine punishment but an extraterrestrial intervention? According to this interpretation, the flood may have been an attempt by advanced beings to erase traces of a prior, highly developed civilization—one that built the pyramids as part of its technological legacy.

Supporters of this theory note that submerged pyramids have been found around the world.[478] Off the coast of Cuba, structures resembling pyramids lie thousands of feet below the ocean surface. In Rock Lake, Wisconsin, researchers have located at least ten pyramid-shaped formations beneath the water, two of which have been mapped with sonar. Similar submerged monuments have been reported in China, Alaska, Bosnia, and Japan. Despite mounting evidence, governments have often denied their existence or restricted access to these sites.

Section 8: Precision Stones of Puma Punku

Discovered in the mid-16th century, Puma Punku—now part of the Tiahuanaco (or Tiwanaku) site—is an anonymous archaeological complex, containing no inscriptions or depictions of people.[479] According to Tsoukalos, it is "the most mysterious site on Earth, eclipsing the pyramids of Giza."[480]

The site features enormous, precisely cut stone blocks, some weighing up to 800 tons, which interlock with puzzle-like precision and display smooth, machine-like surfaces and grooves. Each stone is cut with remarkable accuracy and designed to interlock seamlessly with the surrounding stones, forming load-bearing joints without the use of mortar.[481]

One particularly notable andesite block features a perfect groove with evenly spaced holes drilled along it. Because andesite is too hard to be cut with copper tools, this raises questions about the methods used in its construction.[482] While there is no evidence that laser or plasma tools—or any other heat-based technologies—were employed, the surface of the stones suggests they may have been shaped using a diamond saw or diamond mill.[483] The smoothness of the cuts is astonishing; Tsoukalos describes the surface as being "like touching a bathroom mirror."[484]

The question of how these massive stone platforms were transported remains unresolved. Some researchers have proposed that wooden rollers were used, but this theory presents a major problem: Tiahuanaco lies at an elevation of over 12,500 feet, far above the natural tree line. Because trees do not grow at this altitude, no wood would have been available for rollers, leaving the means by which these stones were transported and shaped unexplained.[485]

Mainstream archaeologists date the construction of Puma Punku to between 536 and 600 CE. However, Tsoukalos argues that the site "might date back as far as 12,000 BCE—about 14,000 years ago."[486] Many of the monuments feature symbols believed to form part of a calendar system. According to Dr. Arthur Posnansky, a distinguished archaeologist, this calendar indicates that the monuments are at least 10,000 years old, with some calculations suggesting dates as early as 17,000 years ago.[487]

Ground-penetrating radar has revealed multiple stone blocks buried up to twelve feet underground, implying that a significant amount of soil has accumulated over time. This evidence suggests the possibility of a cataclysmic event that covered the site.[488]

Local Aymara traditions tell of gods who descended from the sky and jump-started civilization in the region. While many dismiss such stories as mythology, Tsoukalos argues that myths often contain elements of historical truth.[489]

Tsoukalos concludes that Puma Punku was built directly by extraterrestrials.[490] He believes that while these beings did not physically construct the site themselves, they commissioned the Aymara people, sharing advanced engineering knowledge to complete the work. Today, Puma Punku lies in ruins. Tsoukalos speculates that this destruction may have resulted from a cataclysmic event or that the site was intentionally dismantled by its original extraterrestrial builders before they left Earth.[491]

Section 9: *Stargate* and *Alien vs. Predator*

Stargate (1994) builds its story around the "ancient astronaut" hypothesis—the idea that extraterrestrials influenced early human civilization. Throughout the film, references to a time roughly 10,000 years ago, particularly in the dialogue of Dr. Daniel Jackson and Colonel Jack O'Neil, anchor this concept within the movie's mythology and align it with themes of alternative archaeology.

Dr. Jackson (James Spader) claims that the Egyptian pyramids predate recorded history, suggesting they were built around 10,000 years ago rather than during Egypt's Old Kingdom of the 4th dynasty around 2500 BCE. His theory mirrors unorthodox ideas from authors like Erich von Däniken and Graham Hancock, who propose that advanced beings—possibly aliens—guided ancient construction. In the film, Jackson's radical claim is vindicated when the Stargate reveals that an alien posing as the sun god Ra once ruled Earth and used the device for interplanetary travel.

Colonel O'Neil's (Kurt Russell) later discussion of hieroglyphics dating back to the same era reinforces this ancient timeline, connecting both Earth and alien worlds to a shared prehistoric past. The choice of 10,000 years is not random; it aligns with real-world events such as the end of the Younger Dryas, the dawn of agriculture, and the construction of early monumental sites like Göbekli Tepe.

By setting its mythos in this distant epoch, *Stargate* blends science fiction with speculative archaeology, transforming legitimate prehistoric milestones into evidence of alien intervention. The film thus reimagines human origins through a cosmic lens—where the mysteries of ancient civilization are not purely human achievements, but remnants of contact with beings from the stars.

Similarly, *Alien vs. Predator* (2004) extends the ancient astronaut motif, suggesting that another extraterrestrial species—Predators—interacted with humans in prehistory. A Weyland Industries expedition uncovers a buried pyramid beneath Antarctica, revealing that humans become prey in a ritual hunt between Predators and Xenomorphs. The film implies that an ancient, ice-free Antarctica once hosted the first pyramid, constructed by the Predator race as a ceremonial arena for hunting Xenomorphs for sport.

Ancient inscriptions depict humans who worshipped the Predators as gods, unwillingly sacrificing themselves to breed the Xenomorphs used in these sacred rites. This framing suggests that the Predators have visited Earth for millennia, shaping human history and culture through both fear and reverence. Like *Stargate*, the narrative merges myth and archaeology, blending real-world enigmas with speculative interpretations of human-alien contact.

This raises the unsettling possibility that humanity may have long existed under the scrutiny and manipulation of an alien race, enslaved and subject to their whims. According to Firestone, we may be living in what could now be considered the era of the so-called "sixth extinction," echoing the ancient interplay between humans and otherworldly forces depicted in both films.[492]

Section 10: Dr. Steven M. Greer—*Disclosure*

Dr. Steven M. Greer is one of the world's most well-known and influential UFOlogists. He founded the Disclosure Project in 1993, an initiative aimed at advocating increased government transparency regarding UFOs and extraterrestrial phenomena. While it's important to discern—not discount—claims about extraterrestrial encounters, Greer's work continues to serve as a major reference point in the broader discussion of UFO disclosure. For this reason, I draw on two of his most significant works: *Disclosure* (2001) and *Unacknowledged* (2017), the latter of which was adapted into a widely viewed documentary.

Greer's *Disclosure: Military and Government Witnesses Reveal the Greatest Secrets in Modern History*—first published in May 2001—stands as a foundational work in the modern UFO and extraterrestrial disclosure movement. Compiled from over 120 hours of recorded testimony from more than 100 witnesses, the book condenses 33 hours of transcribed material into a nearly 600-page volume.[493]

Disclosure features testimonies from high-ranking military personnel, government insiders, intelligence officers, and corporate contractors. Greer states:

> The search for truth regarding these secret projects has brought me to heads of state, royalty, CIA officials, NSA operatives, U.S. and foreign military leaders, political figures, and high-tech corporate contractors.[494]

These witnesses collectively claim direct or indirect involvement in covert operations and classified programs connected to unidentified flying objects (UFOs), non-human intelligences, and the reverse engineering of extraterrestrial technologies.

Building on the testimony of these individuals, Greer synthesizes their claims into a broader, unified conclusion about the nature and implications of the phenomenon. Greer asserts:

> UFOs are real; they are of extraterrestrial origin; they have been around for decades (if not centuries); there is no evidence that they are hostile; there is probably more than one type of life form visiting us; and aspects of the government have known this for at least 50 years.[495]

Disclosure's central message is clear: humanity is not alone in the universe, and this has been deliberately concealed from the public for generations.

According to Greer, the evidence and testimonies in *Disclosure* support several key assertions:[496]

- Advanced extraterrestrial civilizations have been visiting Earth for a considerable period of time.

- These visitations are part of highly classified, compartmentalized programs within the United States and other governments.

- Extraterrestrial Vehicles (ETVs)—have been downed, recovered, and studied since at least the 1940s, and possibly as early as the 1930s.

- The examination of these vehicles, along with human discoveries dating back to figures like Nikola Tesla, has led to major technological breakthroughs in energy and propulsion.

- These breakthroughs are based on a form of physics that does not rely on fossil fuels or ionizing radiation, allowing for the generation of unlimited clean energy.

- Ultra-classified projects already possess functioning antigravity propulsion systems and advanced energy technologies that, if declassified and applied peacefully, could revolutionize human civilization—eliminating poverty, environmental harm, and energy scarcity.

Greer states that insiders and scientists are prepared to testify in open Congressional hearings about the existence of these classified energy technologies.[497] These technologies, he claims, access the "ever-present quantum vacuum energy" field to produce immense amounts of clean energy without pollution.[498] He stresses that they "are *not* perpetual motion machines" and do not violate the laws of thermodynamics; rather, they harness an ambient energy field that exists all around us.[499]

Many witnesses also claim that governments have recovered extraterrestrial craft and engaged in long-term efforts to reverse engineer their propulsion systems and energy sources. Collectively, these testimonies offer an unprecedented glimpse into alleged classified programs involving extraterrestrial phenomena, advanced technology, and global secrecy.

Among the many voices in *Disclosure,* three stand out for their credibility and far-reaching implications: Commander Graham Bethune, Doctor Carol Rosin, and Sergeant Clifford Stone.

Section 11: Bethune and Anomalous Aerial Vehicles[500]

Commander Graham Bethune, a former U.S. Navy pilot who transported high-ranking officials, recounts a mid-20th-century incident over the Atlantic Ocean. In his testimony, he recounts flying a group of VIPs and fellow pilots into Argentia, Newfoundland, in 1951, when they encountered a 300-foot-wide UFO that shot 10,000 feet straight up in a fraction of a second—directly toward their aircraft—before it suddenly reversed course and vanished.

The event was confirmed by radar and documented in reports by multiple members of the flight crew.[501] In Bethune's own words:

> All of a sudden, we saw, on the water, a yellow halo that
> was very, very small, about 15 miles away. And it came up
> to 10,000 feet like that—a fraction of a second. And I
> thought that it was going to go right through us. So, I
> disengaged the autopilot, pushed the nose over, because I
> was going to go under it at the angle that it was coming

toward me... [It] was anywhere from 250 to 350 feet in diameter... The radar report ... said it was [traveling] 1,800 miles an hour... My boss found the report in the Archives in Wright-Patterson in *Project Blue Book* after talking to Colonel Watson, and he confirmed the speed of 1,800 miles an hour.[502]

Bethune's account underscores that encounters with anomalous aerial vehicles are not limited to public observers; they have been documented by trained military personnel under tightly controlled conditions. His story adds weight to the argument that such phenomena are real, tangible, and have long been monitored by national security agencies.

Section 12: Rosin and Wernher von Braun

Doctor Carol Rosin offers a markedly different, yet equally powerful, perspective. A former aerospace executive of Fairchild Industries and spokesperson for Wernher von Braun—the father of modern rocket science—she recounts his 1974 warnings about a plan to justify space weaponization by hoaxing an extraterrestrial threat.

According to Rosin, von Braun predicted a sequence of fabricated threats that would be used to justify the militarization of space: first communism, then terrorism, followed by rogue nations, asteroids, and finally an alien invasion.[503] He referred to this final scenario as "the last card"—a false-flag operation designed to consolidate global control.[504]

Von Braun, as relayed by Rosin, believed that space should remain free of weapons and that the public should be made aware of the true intentions behind strategies to weaponize space, which he described as "scare tactics."[505] In Rosin's own words:

I have concluded [after 26 years, and now in 1990] that it is based on a few people making a lot of money and gaining power. It is about ego... It isn't about using technology to solve problems and heal people on the planet... It is about a few people who really are playing an old, dangerous, costly game for their own pocketbooks and power struggles... [T]here are a lot of people who actually believe that Armageddon should happen, so we have to have these wars... [W]hen I hear that there is a possible threat of extraterrestrials, and I look at this history of thousands of years of possible ET visitations,... I know it is a lie... The ETs have not taken us away yet. We are still here after thousands of years of visits. If, in fact, they are still visiting us now and we have not been harmed, then we have to look at this as something that is not a hostile occurrence... They are clearly not hostile. We are here.[506]

Rosin's testimony shifts the focus from direct encounters and technology to the political and ideological frameworks that may exploit extraterrestrial phenomena for military or corporate gain.

Section 13: Stone and the "Battle of Los Angeles"

Sergeant Clifford Stone, a retired U.S. Army sergeant, has provided one of the most extraordinary testimonies regarding extraterrestrial encounters. He served in covert military units tasked with recovering crashed extraterrestrial craft—and even living non-human entities.[507] According to Stone, these missions operated outside standard military command structures under deeply compartmentalized black operations.[508]

Stone references a real-life incident from February 1942, just weeks after the attack on Pearl Harbor. Commonly known as the "Battle of Los Angeles," the event involved 15 to 20 unidentified flying objects spotted over the city. U.S. anti-aircraft defenses opened fire but failed to bring down any of the objects.[509]

Stone remarks that this mysterious encounter prompted General Douglas MacArthur to establish the Interplanetary Phenomena Research

Unit, acknowledging that what was observed appeared to be of non-Earth origin—possibly visitors from another planet observing World War II.[510] The 2011 film *Battle: Los Angeles* was loosely inspired by this event.

Section 14: *Independence Day* and Fear-Based Narratives

Such incidents, as noted above in Rosin's testimony, align with what Wernher von Braun reportedly warned about: a long-term strategy of using "scare tactics" to justify the militarization of space. For instance, the 1996 and 2016 films *Independence Day* and *Independence Day: Resurgence* present extraterrestrials as hostile invaders, reinforcing a fear-based narrative that may misrepresent the true nature of these encounters.

Most strikingly, Stone challenges conventional thinking about space travel. In Stone's own words:

> NASA says it is going to take another 1,400 years before we achieve interstellar travel. I'm telling you by the end of this [20th] century, we will be doing that. But if we do nothing to grow spiritually, then we will not achieve interstellar travel. They will stop us. What's worse is that they will make themselves known to an unsuspecting people on this planet... The ETs will do this in order to stop us from going out into space as a threat.[511]

Stone maintains that multiple species of extraterrestrials have been in contact with various governments—not only the U.S.—and that their presence on Earth is driven by scientific and humanitarian purposes.[512] "ETs are not hostile," he insists.[513]

Stone reports visiting locations where craft of unknown origin had landed, stating he personally saw "living and dead bodies of entities" not born on this planet.[514] "We have contact with aliens," he says, "originating from some other solar system. They are not hostile toward us."[515] He adds that humanity must recognize "we are not alone—that we have people from other planets, from other solar systems coming here."[516]

Stone emphasizes the similarities rather than the differences between humans and these beings. They have a perception of God, families, and social cultures.[517] They experience likes and dislikes, think, and feel. "These are real people," he states. "You can call them entities or creatures, but they are just like you and me, and we need to seek out the similarities."[518]

Section 15: Beneath the Pentagon—A *Matrix Reloaded* Reality

Stone alleges that the Pentagon conceals advanced infrastructure beneath its surface. He claims there are multiple underground levels connected by a monorail system, featuring "bullet cars" that seat four passengers—two in the front and two in the back—which travel between various government facilities.[519]

The walls, he says, are not truly walls but hidden doors that open to secret rooms.[520] Stone recounts an incident in which a man shoved him against a wall, revealing a concealed door.[521] Behind it, he says, he found a field table—and beyond that, a "little grey alien," a little over three to three and a half feet tall, as these entities are often reported to be.[522]

What if beneath the Earth's surface lie not only secret bases but entire tunnel systems leading to underground cities and thriving vegetation— home to alien beings who have lived alongside us for millions of years?

The scene Stone describes suggests the hidden passageways in the 2003 film, *The Matrix Reloaded,* where backdoors allow programs to move through the Matrix outside conventional boundaries. Similarly, these secret routes mirror how a select few in government—armed with wealth and influence—operate within a hidden vacuum of power and secrecy.

Like Rosin, Stone argues that extraterrestrial technology could transform life on Earth, particularly in energy production, but remains suppressed to protect existing power structures. His testimony is detailed and emotional, reflecting a profound concern for the ethical consequences of long-standing secrecy.

Together, these three testimonies highlight the diversity and gravity of the disclosures presented in Greer's book. Bethune's experience underscores the legitimacy of UFO encounters as real, observable events involving credible witnesses. Rosin exposes a more strategic—and potentially dystopian—dimension, in which the UFO narrative could be weaponized to advance geopolitical agendas. Stone emphasizes the hidden technological potential and ethical dilemmas surrounding secrecy.

Whether regarded as literal truth or as prompts for critical inquiry, these testimonies challenge conventional views and invite deeper examination of what governments may know—and why they choose to keep it hidden.

Greer argues that the implications of these suppressed technologies are profound. According to multiple accounts that he presents, breakthroughs in energy generation—particularly in "zero-point or free energy"—could have rendered fossil fuels and nuclear power obsolete decades ago.[523]

The potential release of such technology, Greer suggests, could eliminate poverty, solve the climate crisis, and usher in a new era of technological advancement that would enable human civilization to "achieve true sustainability."[524]

However, these possibilities remain unrealized due to an entrenched system of secrecy maintained by powerful interests within the military-industrial complex. These interests, he claims, are motivated by the desire to preserve geopolitical dominance, economic control, and the centralized energy economy.[525]

Greer predicted in 2001 that, if action were taken immediately, global poverty could be effectively eliminated by 2030.[526] Now, just a few years away from that target, such an outcome unfortunately seems unlikely. Presidents such as Jimmy Carter were reportedly denied access to or control over "black projects" due to what Greer describes as a pervasive "vacuum of secrecy."[527]

In *Disclosure,* Greer contends that secrecy on this scale is no longer defensible—ethically, scientifically, or environmentally. He urges readers to recognize the transformative potential of what has been hidden and to become active participants in demanding truth and accountability from their governments. Greer challenges conventional narratives not only about extraterrestrial life but also about power, secrecy, and the future direction of human civilization.

Section 17: The ODNI Report and the New Terminology

On June 25, 2021, the Office of the Director of National Intelligence (ODNI) released the *Preliminary Assessment: Unidentified Aerial Phenomena,* formerly acknowledging the existence of unidentified aerial phenomena (UAPs).[528]

The report examined 144 events between November 2004 and March 2021—of which 143 remained unexplained. According to the assessment, these phenomena could pose a potential "threat" to U.S. military operations and national security, presenting significant "challenges" to defense capabilities.[529] However, some experts have questioned the motivations behind such official concern. As noted by Wernher von Braun and Dr. Carol Rosin, the U.S. government has allegedly fabricated extraterrestrial threats as part of a long-standing "scare tactic," intended to justify the weaponization of space under the guise of national defense.

The terminology surrounding these phenomena has evolved over time. Most people are familiar with the term UFO—unidentified flying object—but this term has increasingly become associated with extraterrestrial life in the public imagination. To address the bias this connotation introduces, the U.S. government and military have rebranded the term as UAP.[530]

Dr. Jon Kosloski, head of the Pentagon's UAP Task Force, explains that "UAP" now stands for unidentified anomalous phenomenon, a broader classification.[531] While "Unidentified Aerial Phenomena" typically refers to unexplained objects or events observed in the sky, commonly used in military and defense contexts, the updated term—unidentified anomalous phenomena—includes phenomena occurring not just in the air but also in space, under the sea, or across other domains.[532] This distinction depends on the user's perspective and the scope of the investigation.

According to Kosloski, the shift in terminology is essential for maintaining objectivity. He states:

> By definition, unidentified and anomalous mean we don't yet know what we're dealing with. It could be any number of things, and we need to approach it without preconceived notions. If we automatically assume it's extraterrestrial, our investigation becomes biased. The shift to 'UAP' helps create distance from that assumption and allows for a more objective analysis.[533]

Kosloski emphasizes that the terminology change is not merely semantic; it reflects a deliberate effort to maintain objectivity and scientific rigor in the study of aerial phenomena.

Section 18: Dr. Steven M. Greer—*Unacknowledged*

The 2017 book *Unacknowledged: An Exposé of the World's Greatest Secret*, adapted into a documentary film of the same name and produced by Greer, explores claims that advanced energy technologies capable of providing unlimited, clean power have been discovered and withheld from the public to protect existing economic and energy systems.

These technologies are said to harness energy from the quantum vacuum and could eliminate the need for fossil fuels. Greer also discusses alleged government secrecy surrounding extraterrestrial contact, underground facilities, incidents where unidentified craft reportedly interfered with nuclear weapons, and much more.

Greer presents three main objectives in *Unacknowledged*, which he outlines as follows:[534]

- **Evidence of hidden events.** To provide evidence supporting a timeline of covert actions that led to the "greatest cover-up in human history." Tens of thousands—if not millions—of extraterrestrial species have visited Earth for a long time. They are not a threat to us; rather, we pose a threat to them, to ourselves, and to our planet's survival through our destructive actions.

- **Expose the Military Industrial Complex.** To reveal how the Cold War gave rise to a covert "government within the government"—a cabal—illegally diverting an estimated \$80–100 billion annually (as of 2017) in taxpayer funds into Unacknowledged Special Access Projects (USAPs) without congressional oversight.

- **Release suppressed technologies.** To disclose zero-point-energy and anti-gravitic systems—technologies that, as a game-changer, could eliminate hunger, poverty, and climate change. These technologies trace back to the Roswell crash landings of June–July 1947.

Section 19: Zero-Point Energy and Free Energy

One of the most prominent themes in *Unacknowledged* is the existence and suppression of zero-point-energy (ZPE) technologies, which are said to have made interstellar travel possible.[535]

Greer maintains that energy devices derived from extraterrestrial sources—capable of extracting power from the quantum vacuum—could provide every home, business, and vehicle with its own source of abundant, free energy—eliminating the need for oil, gas, coal, or nuclear power plants and even roads, since such devices could generate an anti-gravity effect for above-surface transport (i.e., "flying cars") all without producing pollution.[536]

Harnessing this energy source, Greer argues, dates back to Nikola Tesla, who recognized that nature (and electricity) prefers to operate in four dimensions—the fourth being time-space.[537]

By applying a high-voltage system to an electromagnetic field in a counter-rotating vortex, Tesla discovered that a stream of electrons could flow indefinitely through a vacuum at the speed of light without significant loss because the vacuum offered no resistance, essentially incorporating the fourth dimensional aspects of zero-point-energy.[538] This concept later became central to broader discussions surrounding the history and development of zero-point energy throughout the past century.[539]

According to Greer, in 1901, as Tesla was gearing up to reveal his groundbreaking discovery—one that promised free energy and the potential to transform the world—wealthy industrialist J.P. Morgan intervened.[540] Believing free energy violated American capitalist values, Morgan persuaded his contacts in Washington to confiscate Tesla's papers and inventions, leaving Tesla financially ruined.[541]

Greer asserts that every scientist who has created an over-unity device has been "bought out, shut down, or silenced (killed)."[542] U.S. patent law, he claims, enables the government to seize technologies under national security orders.[543] By the end of 2010, Greer alleged that 5,135 inventions had been confiscated and further stated that "free energy systems *already exist*... [and] all the hundreds of trillions of dollars in assets in coal, oil, [and] uranium are obsolete."[544]

In response, Greer created *New Earth Incubator Fund*—an open-source research and development initiative for zero-point-energy operating without patents or intellectual property restrictions.[545] In his words (2017):

> The Earth, if we are lucky, may have the twenty years
> needed to develop this new energy technology, productize
> it, and get it into widespread use globally... Damage already
> done to the planet over the past 150 years of
> industrialization can be rapidly repaired... When energy

costs drop to effectively zero, recycling can approach 100%.[546]

Greer contends that disclosure of such technologies would destabilize global energy markets and undermine centralized economic control—an outcome powerful stakeholders will not permit.

Section 20: Trans-Dimensional Interstellar Science

In 2013, Greer spoke at the National Press Club in Washington, D.C., from April 29 to May 3. During his testimony, he remarked that civilizations millions of years more advanced than ours would appear "magical and incomprehensible"—much like an iPhone would seem like magic to someone from Thomas Jefferson's era, or even more so during the Salem witch trials, where you'd "likely be burned at the stake as a witch."[547] He emphasized that this is why humility is crucial when contemplating our place in the universe.

With roughly 400 billion star systems in the Milky Way, Greer suggests that some advanced civilizations may be capable of interstellar travel.[548] This field of inquiry is known as Trans-Dimensional Interstellar Science (TDIS), which explores advanced phenomena at the intersection of "electromagnetism, magnetic fields, gravitational forces, and three-dimensional space-time" through a central nexus.[549] He notes that elements of this science, including aspects related to consciousness, have already been explored in engineering laboratories at Princeton.[550]

According to Greer, such civilizations are not traveling at light speed—it's "far too slow."[551] But how can these civilizations communicate across vast distances when even light-speed is inadequate? Greer's answer: "thinking is the best way to travel."[552] The speed of thought isn't quantifiable. New physics suggests the ability to teleport across vast distances instantly—something already demonstrated with particles. These civilizations can do it with entire spacecraft and their occupants.[553] Their communication devices—and even their own innate abilities—allow for "thought-actuated events."[554]

Section 21: Underground Extraterrestrial Bases

Among the more extraordinary claims are those involving underground extraterrestrial bases allegedly constructed by private contractors—such as the Bechtel Corporation—on behalf of the U.S. government and military.[555] These bases were reportedly built using nuclear-powered boring machines capable of drilling through and "glassifying" bedrock, leaving no rubble behind.[556]

According to accounts presented by Greer, these underground facilities house alien craft and extraterrestrial biological entities (EBEs), while certain above-ground sites contain "reverse-engineered aircraft" or alien reproduction vehicles (ARVs).[557] The operations of these bases, carried out through top-secret programs, are enabled by several Unacknowledged Special Access Projects (USAPs), involving multiple private corporate entities.[558]

These projects are believed to operate with an annual "black budget" estimated between $80 and $100 billion, and have used trillions of dollars in taxpayer funds over the past seven decades (as of 2017), all without congressional oversight.[559] Greer states that individuals involved in USAPs receive "in excess of $10 million in bribes each" to maintain secrecy.[560]

Recruitment into such highly classified programs—such as the National Reconnaissance Organization (NRO)—allegedly requires a clearance level "38 levels above top secret," a level no U.S. president is said to have ever held.[561] These secret bases are reportedly located in remote areas and connected by extensive subterranean tunnel networks.[562] Trains traveling at "super-high speeds" are said to link one base to another—for example, a tunnel between Dulce and Los Alamos, covering approximately 82 miles, which would take just 15 to 20 minutes to traverse.[563]

Equally dramatic are the testimonies involving extraterrestrial interactions with nuclear facilities.[564] Greer asserts that the mass arrival of UFOs during World War II was no coincidence, emphasizing that Roswell Air Force Base in New Mexico attracted particular attention because it was, at the time, the only unit in the world equipped with atomic weapons.[565]

According to Greer, UFO sightings in New Mexico increased after the atomic bombs were dropped on Hiroshima and Nagasaki.[566] He further notes that the first nuclear weapons were developed at Los Alamos and tested at Alamogordo and the White Sands Missile Range, all located in New Mexico.[567]

Greer maintains that the events at Roswell did, in fact, occur. He reports that the "three so-called flying saucers" recovered were found in New Mexico because, according to an FBI memorandum, "the government has a very high-powered radar set up in that area, and it is believed the radar interferes with the controlling mechanism of the saucers."[568] However, Greer alleges that the weapon activated at Roswell's base was more likely a "scalar or longitudinal wave" system, which he claims is not limited to the speed of light but instead "travels at multiples of the speed of light."[569]

By 1947, Greer contends, the U.S. military was already capable of producing an "effective electromagnetic weapon" through experiments with such systems.[570] Two of the crashed UFOs were reportedly recovered immediately, while the third was located several years later.[571]

In several of these reports, nuclear weapons were allegedly rendered inoperative by these unidentified craft. These incidents include UFO flyovers that led to the shutdown of nuclear missiles inside their silos, as well as the reported interception by UFOs of an intercontinental ballistic missile designed for detonation on the Moon—an interception that occurred before the missile could exit Earth's atmosphere.[572]

Section 23: Peaceful Visitors and the Silence of the Stars

Greer interprets this as evidence that extraterrestrial visitors are peaceful, suggesting they are concerned about humanity's nuclear capabilities and may be attempting to prevent large-scale destruction.[573] This narrative suggests a pattern of extraterrestrial intervention designed to protect life on Earth or possibly to prevent humanity from threatening other parts of the cosmos. This not only implies a protective or regulatory role for extraterrestrials but also offers a possible explanation for the Fermi paradox.

Section 24: The Fermi Paradox

The "fermi paradox" highlights a fundamental contradiction between the high probability of extraterrestrial civilizations in the universe and the complete lack of evidence for their existence.

The Milky Way contains an estimated 400-billion-star systems, most of which are believed to host planets. On average, each system may contain between one and five planets, suggesting that our galaxy alone could contain between 400 billion and 2 trillion planets. When considering that the observable universe contains hundreds of billions to possibly two trillion galaxies, the total number of potential planets becomes almost unimaginable—reaching into the sextillions and highlighting the vast potential for life beyond Earth.

If intelligent civilizations had emerged on even a fraction of these planets, they could have colonized the galaxy in a relatively short span of cosmic time. Yet we find no clear signs—no spacecraft, no radio signals, and no megastructures—raising the question of why the galaxy appears so quiet.

Section 25: Critical Thinking Through the UFO Debate

It seems plausible that extraterrestrial intelligence could be peaceful, intervening only when humanity faces the risk of large-scale destruction, such as nuclear conflict. Current levels of human consciousness, however, may limit the ability to communicate with them through thought.

Drawing on this material, I taught a semester-long Reasoning and Logic course at a local university near the end of the last decade, incorporating two documentaries to explore analogical reasoning and argument analysis.

The first documentary, *Did We Land on the Moon?*, examined conspiracy theories and the structure of skeptical arguments. The second, *Unacknowledged* by Greer, served as a basis for discussing appeals to authority and the evaluation of expert testimony.

To further critique deference to authority, the course also incorporated *South Park's* Eric Cartman and his infamous "Respect My Authoritah" catchphrase as a humorous but pointed lens on how figures such as teachers, political leaders, the Internet, and the media are often treated as unquestionable sources of knowledge.

If Greer's account is true, the implications of the claims presented in *Unacknowledged* are profound. They suggest a world in which humanity already has access to clean, limitless energy but remains shackled to outdated systems through political and economic manipulation and greed. The existence of extraterrestrial life and advanced civilizations would challenge fundamental assumptions in science, religion, and philosophy.

CHAPTER 8
What Does It All Mean?

This book does not claim to offer definitive answers. It invites readers to examine how answers are formed—how systems of knowledge shape the human mind, and how the shaped mind, in turn, sustains those systems.

The chapters move across disciplines, ideas, and controversies, sometimes pausing briefly, sometimes probing more deeply. Endnotes are provided not to overwhelm, but to encourage continued inquiry. What we call knowledge is never final. It remains provisional, sustained by interpretation, defended by institutions, and filtered through the habits of thought we inherit. To think freely requires suspending premature certainty, remaining open to revision, and recognizing how easily the human mind confuses coherence with truth.

Friedrich Nietzsche suggests that embracing multiple perspectives loosens the grip of rigid systems that claim certainty, replacing them with a more expansive spirit—an "air of heights."[574] When we move beyond a single perspective, we enter the "open sea"—becoming a "discoverer" of a "great health," and encountering the vastness of an "undiscovered country," filled with what is beautiful, questionable, frightening, and divine.[575] The metaphor is fitting: to question a system is to leave the safety of the shore. Yet only in open waters does genuine discovery become possible.

This book calls for intellectual humility, curiosity, and disciplined skepticism. It asks not merely whether certain claims are true or false, but how the frameworks through which we interpret them shape what we are able—or willing—to see. That question forms the through-line of this work.

Section 1: Idols in Motion

Bacon's Idols are not mere relics of early modern philosophy, but active concepts for understanding how the human mind is shaped by systems of authority, language, identity, and human nature—and warnings that these influences continue to shape contemporary thought.

Idols of the Theater reveal how authority establishes legitimate knowledge and shapes the boundaries of thought, transforming ideas into belief. Idols of the Marketplace show how language governs the use of words and subtly directs interpretation, constraining thought prior to critical awareness. Idols of the Cave demonstrate how identity, anchored in personal experience, narrows perspective and produces bias. Idols of the Tribe illustrate how human nature inclines us toward consensus, familiarity, and conformity, weakening independent judgment.

These idols are embedded within us. They operate before we recognize them. They shape the human mind before we become aware of them.

Skepticism, when applied to this book, *Systems of Science*, should properly function as a method of inquiry—testing, questioning, and remaining receptive to evidence. But when skepticism hardens into reflexive dismissal, it ceases to be inquiry and becomes another performance of certainty. In such moments, the system defends itself through the mind it has already shaped.

Section 2: Origins, Catastrophes, and Frameworks

In examining theories of human origins—abiogenesis, creationism, natural selection, and panspermia—this book does not ask readers to accept any single account uncritically. Instead, it asks how these frameworks are constructed, defended, and institutionalized.

Abiogenesis, the dominant scientific model for the emergence of life, differs greatly from Aristotle's ancient idea of spontaneous generation. Yet both reflect attempts to explain how life arises from nonliving matter. The difference lies not only in method and evidence, but in the systems that validate and sustain those explanations.

When we turn to catastrophic events—the Younger Dryas, near-extinction scenarios, global flood hypotheses, impact theories—we confront a deeper question: are prevailing scientific frameworks fully equipped to accommodate disruption? Or, like pre-Copernican astronomy, do they sometimes resist revision because they are woven into institutional authority and intellectual prestige?

When a paradigm becomes central to authority, revising it can feel destabilizing: the Idols of the Theater take institutional form, and those who defend the institutions seek to validate the knowledge that sustains them.

Section 3: When the Timeline Resists Revision

The debates surrounding Göbekli Tepe and pre-agricultural monument building intensify this tension. If complex social organization existed earlier than conventional timelines allow, then the linear progression from hunter-gatherer to farmer to civilization may require reconsideration.

The issue is not whether every alternative hypothesis is correct. The question is whether the prevailing framework permits serious engagement with disruptive evidence. When anomalies are dismissed reflexively rather than examined rigorously, the problem extends beyond science. It becomes institutional, cultural, and psychological.

A system that cannot tolerate anomaly often reveals more about the structure of the human mind than about the evidence itself.

Section 4: Cosmology and the Modern Theater

As this book moves from Earth to the Moon and beyond, the same pattern reappears. In earlier centuries, religious authorities guarded the theater of knowledge. Today, governmental, military, and scientific institutions often control access to data, classification, and public interpretation.

When evidence is filtered through secrecy, ridicule, or appeals to national security, skepticism and dogmatism can become difficult to distinguish. The Idols of the Theater remain active—not merely as a metaphor, but as a mechanism through which authority establishes what counts as legitimate knowledge.

Here, the Baconian question resurfaces with urgency: are certain conclusions rejected because they are false, or because they cannot be accommodated within the existing explanatory system?

The answer may not always be clear. What is clear is that institutional control and cognitive bias reinforce one another. Systems shape the human mind; the shaped mind defends the system.

Section 5: Language and the Boundaries of Inquiry

In the final chapters, emotionally charged topics—extraterrestrial hypotheses, unidentified aerial phenomena, ancient myths, disclosure claims—serve as test cases for intellectual openness.

Whether one ultimately accepts or rejects these claims, their reception reveals how language regulates inquiry. Labels such as "fringe," "conspiracy," or "pseudoscience" can function as linguistic gatekeepers. Once applied, they often end discussion before investigation begins.

In this way, the Idols of the Theater converge with the Idols of the Marketplace. Established intellectual frameworks (theater) shape the vocabulary through which ideas are described, while language itself (marketplace) reinforces those frameworks. Definitions shift, terms narrow or expand, and inquiry is subtly directed toward some conclusions and away from others.

When language closes off questioning in advance, inquiry gives way to agreement. The result is consensus rather than discovery—and consensus, however reassuring, is not synonymous with truth.

Section 6: When the Story Defends Itself

The Scientific Revolution advanced not by rejecting authority wholesale, but by recognizing its limits. Bacon did not call for abandoning systems of knowledge; he called for holding them provisionally, subject to revision in light of new evidence.

Many of today's contentious debates arise not from a lack of data, but from tension between anomalies and entrenched explanatory frameworks. When the evidence challenges the story, the story may adapt—or it may resist.

When resistance occurs, it is often subtle. The story defends itself because the human mind, shaped by the story, experiences revision as threat.

Section 7: What Comes Next?

Book 1, *Systems of Science,* has explored how authoritative frameworks shape interpretation within contemporary inquiry. If something exists beyond what our current understanding suggests, our greatest task may not be to conquer the unknown, but to recognize the limits of our own frameworks.

Ideas exist in the human mind. Yet ideas, once institutionalized, structure the world we inhabit. We do not merely hold frameworks; frameworks hold us.

When our inherited systems are challenged, our instinct is often defensive. But allowing space to consider alternative narratives—without surrendering discernment—expands intellectual freedom. Openness does not require agreement; it requires humility.

Book 2, *Systems of Ideology*, continues by examining how power, justice, and morality are constructed within authority-imposed frameworks. From the Code of Hammurabi to thinkers such as the Buddha, Confucius, Plato, Aristotle, and Machiavelli, and extending to modern philosophers and foundational documents, the book explores how these structured systems of ideas, beliefs, values, and principles shape the ways individuals and groups perceive, interpret, and act in the world.

The books in this volume aim to go beyond comfort, consensus, and the illusion that the theater of belief is identical with truth. They encourage a spirit of inquiry that does not fear change, because change is often the first sign that we have mistaken the theater for truth. When a new or challenging idea disrupts the established framework, it may be because the theater of knowledge has distorted the human mind's experience of reality.

Randy M. Herring holds an M.A. in Philosophy and a B.A. in Religious Studies, with additional study in Exercise Science. He has taught philosophy, ethical theory, and logic at colleges and universities in Eastern Washington. His academic interests include ethics, existentialism, embodiment, epistemology, and the philosophy of human flourishing.

In addition, Randy brings nearly fifty years of experience in bodybuilding and fitness training, grounding his philosophical reflections in lived embodiment. He has lived and worked in Japan and traveled extensively in Israel and Palestine.

Randy is the author of three books, including this one. His work takes a humanistic approach to exploring the many forces that shape the human condition. A three-time cancer survivor, he offers insights into human flourishing, resilience, and the fragile beauty of life.

Endnotes

1   Galileo Galilei, *Letter to the Grand Duchess Christina* (1615), in *Discoveries and Opinions of Galileo.* Translated by Stillman Drake. Anchor Books, 1957, p. 183. Note: The letter is 40 pages long.

2   This use of "nothingness" draws on Jean-Paul Sartre's concept in *Being and Nothingness* (1943), particularly his analysis of self-awareness and bad faith.

3   Aristotle. *Nicomachean Ethics.* In *The Complete Works of Aristotle, Vol. 2.* Edited by Jonathan Barnes. Translated by W.D. Ross. Revised by J.O. Urmson. Princeton University Press. Sixth printing 1995. Book 2, Chapter 1, Lines 1103b24–25 (2.1.1103b24–25), p. 1743. Paraphrased.

4   Identity is referred to as a system because it functions through social roles within specific environments, producing skewed perspectives and reinforcing assumptions (see note 18 below).

5   Human nature is referred to as a system because it emerges within social organization, shaping values and amplifying a collective consensus that appears naturalized—however unnatural it may be—especially in the early twenty-first century (see note 18 below).

6   Galileo, *Dialogue Concerning the Two Chief World Systems* (1632). Translated by Stillman Drake, foreword by Albert Einstein, University of California Press, 1953. Second revised edition, 1967. Copyright renewed 1981. This work is a remarkable piece of literary art, modeled on the Platonic dialogue tradition yet strategically adapted by Galileo to ensure the triumph of the Copernican position. The text is highly engaging, enlivened by Galileo's use of humor, satire, and occasional ridicule—most notably through the character of Simplicio, who embodies the traditional Aristotelian–Ptolemaic worldview. I read the work over the course of two months when I was in my early to mid-40s.

7   Robert C. Solomon and Kathleen M. Higgins, *A Passion for Wisdom: A Very Brief History of Philosophy.* Oxford University Press, 1997, p. 69.

8   John Cottingham, et al. *The Philosophical Writings of Descartes, Volume III: The Correspondence.* Translated by John Cottingham, et al. Cambridge University Press, 1991, p. 40. Abbr. Cottingham.

9   Cottingham, 41.

10   René Descartes. *Treatise on Light* (1633). In *The World and Other Writings.* Translated and edited by Stephen Gaukroger. Cambridge University Press, 1998, p. 46.

11   Cottingham, 41.

12   René Descartes. *Principles of Philosophy* (1644). Translated by Valentine Rodger Miller and Reese P. Miller. Kluwer Academic Publishers, 1991, pp. 94-95.

13   Francis Bacon. *Advancement of Learning* (1605) In *Great Books of the Western World, Vol. 28.* Edited by Mortimer J. Adler. Encyclopaedia Brittanica, Inc. Ninth printing 2007. Book 1, Parts I–II, Sections 3–8 (1.I.3–1.II.8), pp. 2–7. Paraphrased.

14   Francis Bacon, *Novum Organum* (1620). In *Great Books of the Western World, Vol. 28.* Edited by Mortimer J. Adler. Encyclopaedia Brittanica, Inc., 2007. Book 1, Aphorism 3 (1.3), p. 107. Abbr. Bacon, Novum Organum.

15   Bacon, Novum Organum (1.23), 108.

16   Bacon, Novum Organum (1.39), 109.

17   Bacon, Novum Organum (1.39-68), pp. 109-116.

18   Bacon organizes his four idols—the Tribe, Cave, Marketplace, and Theater—as a progression from the most natural and fundamental sources of error to increasingly artificial and cultural ones, moving from internal sources of distortion to external influences. In contrast, my analysis reverses this order, beginning with the most artificial and externally constructed influences and moving toward what eventually appears innate and natural. This progression traces how external structures shape internal perception, moving from external systems to internalized identity and consequently to perceived human nature. Authoritative

institutions establish overarching frameworks shaping systems of knowledge and belief corresponding to the Idol of the Theater. These systems in turn stabilize meanings and determine what counts as legitimate language or structured ways of speaking and thinking, corresponding to the Idol of the Marketplace. Language then shapes how individuals understand themselves, their social roles, and their intellectual outlook, aligning with the Idol of the Cave. Over time, these shared identities become normalized and are interpreted as natural features of humanity, corresponding to the Idol of the Tribe. In this way, the progression can be summarized as authority → language → identity → human nature, illustrating how systems of power and social organization produce and reinforce biases.

[19] D. C. Johanson & M. A. Edey, *Lucy: The Beginnings of Humankind.* New York: Simon and Schuster, 1981.

[20] Agustín Fuentes. *Biological Anthropology: Concepts and Connections, 3rd Edition.* McGraw Hill Education, 2019, p. 217. Abbr. Fuentes.

[21] Fuentes, 217.

[22] Wangiji Hu et al. "Genomic inference of a severe human bottleneck during the Early to Middle Pleistocene transition." *Science* (New York, N.Y.) vol. 381,6661 (2023): 979-984. doi:10.1126/science.abq7487. Abbr. Hu.

[23] Hu, 981.

[24] Hu, 983.

[25] Hu, 983.

[26] Hu, 983.

[27] Hu, 983.

[28] Hu, 983.

[29] Hu, 983.

[30] Fuentes, 256.

[31] Yuval Noah Harari, *Sapiens: A Brief History of Humankind, 10th Anniversary Edition.* HarperCollins Publishers, 2024, pp. 6-7, 14. Abbr. Harari.

[32] Graham Hancock, *America Before: The Key to Earth's Lost Civilization.* St. Martin's Press, New York, 2019, pp. 83-85. Abbr. Hancock, America.

[33] Denisova Cave in Siberia is the site where remains of the enigmatic Denisovans were discovered, first identified in 2008 through DNA analysis of a finger bone. Though genetically distinct from both Neanderthals and modern humans, the classification of Denisovans as a separate species (*Homo denisova*) remains debated due to the scarcity of fossil material and the reliance on genetic data over anatomical evidence.

[34] Fuentes, 256; Harari, 14.

[35] Harari, 14.

[36] Harari, 14-19.

[37] Harari, 16.

[38] Richard E Green et al. "A draft sequence of the Neandertal genome." *Science.* 2010 May 7; 328 (5979): 710-722. doi:10.1126/science.1188021. Retrieved: https://pmc.ncbi.nlm.nih.gov/articles/PMC5100745/pdf/nihms-827403.pdf. Abbr. Green, Neandertal genome.

[39] Fuentes, 256; Harari, 18-19.

[40] Richard Firestone et al, *The Cycle of Cosmic Catastrophes: How a Stone-Age Comet Changed the Course of World Culture.* Bear & Company, 2006, p. 237. Abbr. Firestone.

[41] Firestone, 237.

[42] Firestone, 237.

[43] Firestone, 237.

[44] Firestone, 237-238.

[45] Firestone, 238.

[46] Immanuel Velikovsky, a Russian-born physician and independent scholar who proposed unconventional theories linking ancient history, mythology, and astronomy, adopted a

similar perspective, arguing that Earth's history has been shaped by sudden cosmic disturbances and planetary encounters. While both Velikovsky and Firestone share a broad commitment to catastrophic explanations for historical and geological change, their methods and evidence differ significantly. Velikovsky relies heavily on interpretations of ancient texts and mythologies and are widely rejected by mainstream scientific disciplines. Firestone, by contrast, frames his argument as a scientific hypothesis grounded in physical evidence such as isotopic anomalies, radiocarbon spikes, and geological markers, and his work remains controversial but debated within scientific contexts. See Velikovsky, *Worlds in Collision* (1950). New and unchanged ed., Paradigma Ltd., 2009.

[47] Firestone, 4–8, 43.

[48] Firestone, 238.

[49] Firestone, 238.

[50] Firestone, 238.

[51] Firestone, 239.

[52] Firestone, 240.

[53] Firestone, 240.

[54] Firestone, 240.

[55] Firestone, 240.

[56] Firestone, 240.

[57] Sanja Panovska, "Long-term changes of the geomagnetic field: recent progress, challenges and applications," EGU General Assembly 2024, Vienna, Austria, 14–19 Apr 2024, EGU24-10977. Retrieved: https://doi.org/10.5194/egusphere-egu24-10977. Abbr. Panovska.

[58] Panovska.

[59] Panovska.

[60] Panovska.

[61] Ocean Ramsey is a marine biologist and shark conservationist known for her efforts to protect sharks, particularly in Hawaii. She has worked to raise awareness about the importance of sharks in marine ecosystems and has played a key role in advocating for shark protection laws in Hawaii. She is also the subject of the 2020 Netflix film, *Shark Whisperer.* Prior to that, Ocean appeared in several documentaries.

[62] G.S. Kirk et al. *The Presocratic Philosophers, 2nd Edition.* Cambridge University Press, 1983, p. 177. Abbr. Kirk.

[63] Kirk, 89.

[64] Kirk, 177.

[65] Aristotle. *Generation of Animals.* In *The Complete Works of Aristotle, Vol. 1.* Edited by Jonathan Barnes. Translation by A. Platt. Princeton University Press. Sixth printing 1995. Book 3, Chapter 11, Lines 762a21–762b20 (3.11.762a21–762b20), p. 1180.

[66] Aristotle. *History of Animals.* In *The Complete Works of Aristotle, Vol. 1.* Edited by Jonathan Barnes. Translation by d' A. W. Thompson. Princeton University Press. Sixth printing 1995. Book 5, Chapter 1, Lines 539a21–23 (5.1.539a21–23), p. 852. Abbr. Aristotle, History of Animals. Paraphrased.

[67] Aristotle, History of Animals, (5.19.552a22), 871.

[68] Alexander I. Oparin. *The Origin of Life* (1924). Translated into English by Sergius Morgulis in 1938. Dover Publications, Inc., 1953, pp. 7-11. Abbr. Oparin.

[69] G.E.R. Lloyd, *Aristotle: The Growth and Structure of His Thought.* Cambridge University Press, 1968, p. 61.

[70] Kara Rogers. "abiogenesis." *Encyclopedia Britannica*, 30 Jan. 2026. Retrieved: https://www.britannica.com/science/abiogenesis.

[71] Alan D. Gishlick, "Icons of Evolution? Why Much of What Jonathan Wells Writes about Evolution is Wrong." November 2006. National Center for Science Education. Retrieved: https://ncse.ngo/icon-1-miller-urey-experiment. Abbr. Gishlick.

72 Alka Misra, "Miller-Urey Experiment." Retrieved: https://www.lkouniv.ac.in/site/writereaddata/siteContent/202003291608408879alka_misra_Miller_urey_experiment.pdf. Abbr. Misra.

73 Oparin, 157-158.

74 Oparin, 248.

75 In the excerpt above in the main text, Oparin primarily addresses point (1), but his argument is grounded in a framework that assumes points (2) and (3) as necessary components of life's origins. Oparin's theory became central to the study of life's beginnings. His book, *The Origin of Life,* was later expanded and translated into several languages, significantly influencing the field of origin-of-life studies.

76 Gishlick.

77 Stanley L. Miller. "A Production of Amino Acids Under Possible Primitive Earth Conditions." *Science* (New York, N.Y.) vol. 117,3046 (1953): 528-9. doi:10.1126/science.1173046.528. Abbr. Miller-Urey. See also: https://labs.bio.unc.edu/goldstein/miller1953.pdf.

78 Misra.

79 Misra.

80 Misra.

81 Miller-Urey.

82 See note 77 above.

83 Gishlick.

84 Gishlick.

85 Gishlick.

86 Samuel Enoch Stumpf, *Socrates to Sartre and Beyond: A History of Philosophy, 7th Edition.* McGraw Hill (2003), p. 25.

87 Aristotle. *Metaphysics.* In *The Complete Works of Aristotle, Vol. 2.* Edited by Jonathan Barnes. Translation by W. D. Ross. Princeton University Press 1995, (1.3.984b15-20), p. 1557. Paraphrased.

88 Hilary Gatti's *Giordano Bruno and Renaissance Science* (1999) provides valuable historical context for understanding Bruno's cosmological beliefs and intellectual development, particularly his extension of Copernican astronomy and his ethical approach to scientific discovery.

89 A. Cassan, et al. "One or More Bound Planets per Milky Way Star from Microlensing Observations." *Nature*, 12 Jan. 2012. Retrieved: https://arxiv.org/abs/1202.0903.

90 Genesis 1:27.

91 Thomas Aquinas. *Summa Contra Gentiles, Book One: God* (1261–64). Chapter 26. Translated by Anton C. Pegis. University of Notre Dame Press, 1975.

92 Thomas Aquinas. *Summa Theologiae* (1265). In *Great Books of the Western World, Vol. 17.* Edited by Mortimer J. Adler. Encyclopaedia Brittanica, Inc. Fifth printing 1994. Part I, Question 93, Article 4 (I.93.4), pp. 494-495.

93 Eugenie E. Scott. *Evolution vs. Creationism: An Introduction, 2nd Edition.* University of California Press, 2009, pp. 64-66. Abbr. Scott. Note: *The Open Bible: New King James Version,* Thomas Nelson, Inc., 1983, appears to lean toward a Young Earth Creationist (YEC) view, dating the beginning of Genesis to 4004 BCE "or earlier" (pp. 1–2). In contrast, *The New Catholic Study Bible: St. Jerome Edition,* Thomas Nelson, Inc., 1985, omits any date and reflects an Old Earth Creationist (OEC) perspective, stating: "The time period of chapters 1 through 11 of Genesis takes us back to the very beginning of all things. It must never be forgotten, however, that chapters 1 through 11 are not a scientific account of the beginning of the universe or life" (p. 1).

94 Scott, 68.

95 Scott, 68.

96 Scott, 70.

97 Darwin, however, argues that complexity and intricate design can arise through natural processes.
98 Erich Von Däniken, *Chariots of the Gods, 50th Anniversary Edition.* Translated by Michael Heron. Berkley Books, 2018, p. 4. Abbr. Von Däniken, Chariots.
99 Von Däniken, Chariots, 4.
100 Von Däniken, Chariots, 4.
101 Von Däniken, Chariots, 5.
102 Von Däniken, Chariots, 4-5.
103 Von Däniken, Chariots, 4.
104 Darwin didn't use the word "evolution" in the first edition of *On the Origin of Species.* Instead, he used the phrase "descent with modification" to describe the process by which species change over time. He introduced the term "evolution" in the sixth and final edition of the book, published in 1872, as the term became more common in discussions of his theory.
105 Fuentes, 32-34.
106 Fuentes, 34.
107 Fuentes, 34.
108 Fuentes, 35.
109 Charles Darwin, *On the Origin of Species by Means of Natural Selection or The Preservation of Favoured Races in the Struggle for Life* (1859). Penguin Classics, 1985, p. 134. Abbr. Darwin.
110 Darwin, 147. My emphasis.
111 Darwin, 147.
112 Darwin, 147.
113 Darwin, 96.
114 Darwin, 131-32.
115 Fuentes, 35.
116 Darwin, 342, 404, 435. See note 104 above. Darwin does not use the term "evolution" in the first edition of *On the Origin of Species.*
117 Darwin, 68. His emphasis.
118 Darwin, 90.
119 Darwin, 444.
120 Darwin, 455.
121 Darwin. 458.
122 Darwin, 236.
123 Fuentes, 37.
124 Fuentes, 37.
125 Fuentes, 38.
126 Fuentes, 38.
127 Fuentes, 38.
128 Fuentes, 38.
129 Fuentes, 38.
130 Fuentes, 38.
131 Fuentes, 38.
132 Fuentes, 38-39.
133 Darwin, 459-460.
134 *Prometheus.* Written by Jon Spaihts and Damon Lindelof, directed by Ridley Scott, *Prometheus*, 20th Century Fox, 2012. Retrieved: https://www.scripts.com/script-pdf-body.php?id=16307. Abbr. Prometheus, script.
135 Prometheus, script.
136 Prometheus, script. Due to relativistic effects, approximately 40 years have passed on Earth. This relativistic time effect refers to Einstein's theory of relativity, which states that time slows down for travelers moving at near-light speeds relative to those on Earth. See

Albert Einstein, *Relativity: The Special and General Theory* (1916). Translated by Robert W. Lawson. Pi Press, 2005.

137 Fuentes, 256.

138 Fuentes, 256, 267.

139 Graham Hancock, *Magicians of the Gods.* St Martin's Press, New York, 2015, pp. 22-23. Abbr. Hancock, Magicians.

140 Kirk, 267–378.

141 Oparin, 33-34; 36-43.

142 Philip Coppens, *The Ancient Alien Question.* New Page Books, 2012, p. 199. Abbr. Coppens.

143 A.J. Gentile, *The Why Files,* "We Are the Aliens | Life's Interstellar Journey to Earth: Panspermia." YouTube. 1 Feb. 2024. Retrieved: https://www.youtube.com/watch?v=xxZLBncNRXs&t=1024s. Abbr. Gentile, Panspermia.

144 Gentile, Panspermia.

145 Gentile, Panspermia.

146 Gentile, Panspermia.

147 Gentile, Panspermia.

148 Gentile, Panspermia.

149 Gentile, Panspermia.

150 Gentile, Panspermia.

151 Gentile, Panspermia.

152 Coppens, 200.

153 Gentile, Panspermia.

154 Gentile, Panspermia.

155 Francis H. C. Crick., and Leslie E. Orgel. "Directed Panspermia." *Icarus*, vol. 19, no. 3, 1973, pp. 341–346. Abbr. Crick.

156 Crick, 344.

157 Crick, 344.

158 Crick, 344.

159 Fuentes, 253ff.

160 Fuentes, 253.

161 Von Däniken, Chariots, 30-31.

162 Two main chronologies are proposed for the 430-year period, corresponding to either a 15th-century or a 13th-century Exodus. The *15th-century Exodus* chronology begins in 1875 BCE, when God called Abraham to leave his homeland (Gen. 12:4). Two hundred fifteen years later, in 1660 BCE, Jacob and his family entered Egypt (Gen. 46:21). Another 215 years passed before the Exodus, which is dated to the spring of 1445 BCE and associated with the reign of Pharaoh Amenhotep II. This earlier date is generally accepted by minority conservative Christian groups that favor a literal chronological reading of the biblical text. The *13th-century Exodus* chronology begins with Israel's entry into Egypt in 1660 BCE (Gen. 46:21). In this view, the 430 years of sojourning (Gen. 15:13; Ex. 12:40) are counted entirely from that point, culminating in the Exodus in 1265 BCE during the reign of Pharaoh Ramses II (Ex. 1:11). This later date is widely accepted by Protestant and Catholic scholars who emphasize archaeological evidence and historical-critical analysis of the text. The dates presented here are drawn from personal notes and a chronological timeline developed for a biblical archaeology course, which have been kept in one of my Bibles for nearly forty years.

163 Von Däniken, Chariots, 61.

164 *The Epic of Gilgamesh.* Translated by N.K. Sandars with an Introduction. Penguin Books, 1972, p. 61. Abbr. Gilgamesh.

165 Gilgamesh, 62-69.

166 Gilgamesh, 70-88.

167 Gilgamesh, 89-96. Mainstream scholars commonly translate the term Anunnaki as "the offspring of Anu," the Mesopotamian sky god, referring to a group of deities within the

ancient pantheon. Alternative interpretations, however, render the term as "those from whom the heavens came" or "those who came from the sky," giving rise to speculative theories that identify the Anunnaki as extraterrestrial beings.

[168] Gilgamesh, 97-113.

[169] Gilgamesh, 114-119.

[170] Gilgamesh, Introduction, 22.

[171] Hancock, Magicians, 47-68.

[172] Hancock, Magicians, 55.

[173] Estimates for the emergence of Neanderthals vary. Harari (p. viii) cites approximately 500,000 years ago, while Fuentes (p. 256) suggests a date closer to 300,000 years ago. I have chosen to use 400,000 years ago as a midpoint to reflect the general consensus in paleoanthropology that Neanderthals likely evolved between these dates, depending on definitions and fossil interpretations.

[174] Harari, 14-16.

[175] Green, Neandertal genome.

[176] Harari, 3.

[177] Aristotle. *Politics.* In *The Complete Works of Aristotle, Vol. 2.* Edited by Jonathan Barnes. Translated by B. Jowett. Princeton University Press. Sixth printing 1995. Book 1, Chapter 2, Lines 1253a3 (1.2.1253a3), p. 1987. Paraphrased.

[178] Harari, 22-23.

[179] Harari, 23-24.

[180] Harari, 24.

[181] Harari, 24.

[182] Harari, 56.

[183] Firestone, 24.

[184] Firestone, 8; Hancock, Magicians, 87.

[185] Firestone, 8; Hancock, Magicians, 87.

[186] Firestone, 9.

[187] Hancock, America, 397ff.

[188] Hancock, America, 398.

[189] Hancock, Magicians, 62, 114-15.

[190] Hancock, Magicians, 84.

[191] Hancock, Magicians, 120.

[192] Hancock, Magicians, 65.

[193] Firestone, 144.

[194] Firestone, 313-12; Hancock, Magicians, 69-82.

[195] Hancock, Magicians, 118.

[196] Hancock, Magicians, 76.

[197] Firestone, 144.

[198] Hancock, Magicians, 119-120.

[199] Hancock, America, 375.

[200] Hancock, America, 375.

[201] Hancock, America, 375.

[202] Firestone, 287-88.

[203] Firestone, 36-39, 93, 344; Hancock, America, 377.

[204] In *Timaeus* and *Critias* (360 BCE), Plato places the destruction of Atlantis "nine thousand years" before the time of Solon (640–560 BCE), the Athenian lawmaker and reformer (see note 219 below). This chronological claim is significant for catastrophic theorists, who emphasize sudden, violent events rather than gradual change, as proposed by gradualist theorists. In his *Introduction*, Firestone begins by discussing Plato's account of Atlantis's catastrophic destruction (1). Similarly, in *Magicians of the Gods*, Hancock references Plato, Solon, and the destruction of Atlantis early in the book, at the end of Chapter 1 (33).

205 Hancock, Magicians, 122.

206 Hancock, America, 399.

207 Firestone, 3, 271; Hancock, America, 381.

208 Firestone, 2.

209 For NASA planetary defense (NEO) spending, see:
https://aas.org/posts/news/2025/06/fy26-presidents-budget-request. For U.S. Department of Defense spending, see: https://www.congress.gov/crs-product/IN12447.

210 Hancock, Magicians, 6-7; Harari, 89.

211 Harari, 90.

212 Harari, 91.

213 Harari, 91.

214 Hancock, Magicians, 5, 11, 21-23.

215 Harari, 89.

216 Hancock, Magicians, 7.

217 Hancock, Magicians, 28.

218 Hancock, Magicians, 28-31.

219 Plato, *The Collected Dialogues*, ed. Edith Hamilton and Huntington Cairns. Princeton University Press, 1989, *Timaeus* (22a-25d) pp. 1156-60; *Critias* (108e) pp.1214–15. Abbr. Plato. See also Graham Hancock, *Magicians of the Gods*, p. 33. Interestingly, Plato also describes ancient Egyptian art as literally dating back "ten thousand years ago," which translates to around 10,450 BCE in our calendar (Plato was born around 428 BCE). See *Plato, Laws*, Book II, (656e–657) p. 1254. In *Magicians of the Gods*, Graham Hancock argues that the layout of the Giza pyramids corresponds to the stars of Orion's Belt as they appeared around 10,450 BCE, and that the Sphinx aligns with the constellation Leo during that same epoch. He proposes that prehistoric survivors of a global catastrophe—linked to the Younger Dryas event (12,800–11,600 years ago)—initiated the construction of, or influenced, elements of the Giza complex, particularly the Sphinx and its stellar alignments, which suggest a much older date than conventional Egyptology accepts: around 10,450 BCE. See pp. 188–98ff; 202.

220 Danny Hilman Natawidjaja, *Plato Never Lied: Atlantis Is In Indonesia*, Booknesia, Jakarta, 2013. See also Graham Hancock, *Magicians of the Gods*, Chapter 2.

221 Hancock, Magicians, 239ff, 253, 265, 388.

222 Coppens, 135-36.

223 R.B. Firestone, A. West, J.P. Kennett, et al. "Evidence for an extraterrestrial impact 12,900 years ago that contributed to the megafaunal extinctions and the Younger Dryas cooling." Proceedings of the *National Academy of Sciences of the United States of America* vol. 104,41 (2007): 16016-21. doi:10.1073/pnas.0706977104. Retrieved: https://pmc.ncbi.nlm.nih.gov/articles/PMC1994902/pdf/zpq16016.pdf. See also Firestone et al., *The Cycle of Cosmic Catastrophes* (2006), as cited above.

224 Hancock, Magicians, 234, 287, 300, 438.

225 Hancock, Magicians, 439.

226 Hancock, Magicians, 439.

227 Hancock, Magicians, 429-430.

228 Hancock, Magicians, 438.

229 The 2009 film, *2012* is loosely based on popular interpretations and misinterpretations of the Mayan calendar's 2012 date.

230 Hancock, Magicians, 429-430.

231 Hancock, Magicians, 429, 438.

232 Hancock, Magicians, 429.

233 Neil deGrasse Tyson, *Starry Messenger: Cosmic Perspectives on Civilization*. Henry Holt and Company, New York, 2022, p. 60. Abbr. Tyson, Starry.

234 Tyson, Starry, xiii.

235 Tyson. Starry, xiii.

236 Tyson, Starry, xiv.

237 Tyson, Starry, 45-46.

238 Tyson, Starry, 8-11.

239 Tyson, Starry, 71-72.

240 Tyson, Starry, 24-25.

241 Tyson, Starry, 160.

242 Tyson, Starry, 149.

243 Tyson, Starry, 163.

244 Authur Schopenhauer. *Essays and Aphorisms.* Selected and translated by R.J. Hollingdale. "On the Vanity of Existence." Penguin Classics, 1970, p. 51.

245 Tyson, Starry, 207.

246 Tyson, Starry, 213.

247 Tyson, Starry, 214.

248 Tyson, Starry, 216.

249 Tyson, Starry, 216.

250 Annie Jacobsen, *Nuclear War: A Scenario.* Penguin Random House, 2024, p. xvii. Abbr. Jacobsen. Note: The Sun's core reaches a temperature of 27 million degrees Fahrenheit. Jacobsen gives a conservative—or possibly incorrect—estimate, stating it's "four or five times hotter" than the Sun's core, when it is roughly 6.67 times hotter.

251 Jacobsen, 17.

252 Jacobsen, 166.

253 Jacobsen, 22. Refer to Jacobsen's inset box titled "History Lesson No. 1: Deterrence."

254 Jacobsen, 58-60.

255 Jacobsen, 150.

256 Jacobsen, 282-289. Refer to Jacobsen's inset box titled "History Lesson No. 8: Radiation Sickness" on pages 214-217 for information on the effects of radiation poisoning.

257 Jacobsen, 288.

258 Jacobsen, 277.

259 Jacobsen, 290.

260 Jacobsen, 297.

261 Jacobsen, 290-295.

262 Jacobsen, 295.

263 Jacobsen, 295.

264 Jacobsen, 295.

265 Lex Fridman, "Annie Jacobsen: Nuclear War, CIA, KGB, Aliens, Area 51, Roswell & Secrecy." *Lex Fridman Podcast*, no. 420, 22 Mar. 2024, https://lexfridman.com/annie-jacobsen. Timestamp 01:47:41.

266 Jacobsen, 295-296.

267 Nikolai S. Kardashev. "Transmission of Information by Extraterrestrial Civilizations." *Soviet Astronomy*, vol. 8, no. 2, Sept.–Oct. 1964, pp. 217–221. Translated by the U.S. Office of Technical Services, NASA TT F-677, 1964. SETI Institute. Retrieved: https://technosearch.seti.org/wp-content/uploads/2018-09/Kardashev_CTA102.pdf. Abbr. Kardashev.

268 Kardashev.

269 Michio Kaku, *The Future of Humanity: Terraforming Mars, Interstellar Travel, Immortality, and Our Destiny Beyond Earth.* Doubleday. New York, 2018, p. 250. Abbr. Kaku.

270 Kaku, 250.

271 Coppens, 153.

272 Rick Stroud, *The Book of the Moon.* Walker & Company. New York, 2009, p. 25. Abbr. Stroud.

273 Stroud, 26-27.

274 Stroud, Chapter 6, 259-299.

[275] Stroud, Chapter 8, 339-344.

[276] Stroud, 233.

[277] Hamish Lindsay. "ALSEP: Apollo Lunar Surface Experiments Package," 19 November 1969–30 September 1977. *NASA,* 2008. Retrieved: https://www.nasa.gov/history/alsj/HamishALSEP.html. Abbr. Lindsay.

[278] Lindsay.

[279] Lindsay.

[280] Lindsay.

[281] Lindsay.

[282] National Aeronautics and Space Administration. "Apollo 13 Mission Report." *NASA.* Sept. 1970 (168pp). Retrieved: https://sma.nasa.gov/SignificantIncidents/assets/apollo-13-mission-report.pdf. P. 105. Abbr. Apollo 13 Mission Report.

[283] Apollo 13 Mission Report, 105.

[284] Apollo 13 Mission Report, 105.

[285] Stroud, 318.

[286] Stroud, 318-319. Stroud states that the "body is made up of 80 per cent water," but I changed this to 60%, which is the standard estimate for the average adult human body. The 80% figure more accurately applies to infants or newborns, while lean, muscular adults are closer to 70% and older adults are often nearer 50% because fat contains less water than muscle. For an average adult population, 60% is the more accurate figure Stroud should have cited.

[287] Stroud, 316.

[288] Stroud, 333.

[289] Jean J. Souchay (ed.), *Dynamics of Extended Celestial Bodies And Rings: Lecture Notes in Physics,* Vol. 682, Springer, 2006, p. 159.

[290] Stroud, 332.

[291] Stroud, 331.

[292] Christopher Knight and Alan Butler, *Who Built the Moon?* Originally published in 2005. This edition published by Watkins, United Kingdon, London, 2015. Abbr. Knight and Butler.

[293] Knight and Butler, 4-5.

[294] Isaac Asimov (1920–1992) was a Russian-born American author, biochemist, and professor, best known for his *Foundation* and *Robot* science fiction series. A prolific writer of over 500 books, he also published widely in non-fiction, covering science, history, religion, and literature. Asimov was an outspoken agnostic and humanist and served as president of the American Humanist Association.

[295] Knight and Butler, 56-57.

[296] Knight and Butler, 71-72.

[297] Apollo 13 Mission Report, 105.

[298] Knight and Butler, 71-72.

[299] Apollo 13 Mission Report, 105.

[300] Knight and Butler, 72.

[301] Knight and Butler, 73.

[302] Knight and Butler, 25-31.

[303] Knight and Butler, 26.

[304] Knight and Butler, 215 (see fig. 13). A Möbius strip is a surface with only one side and one edge, making it a key object in topology. To make one, twist a strip of paper 180 degrees and join the ends. Instead of a regular loop, this creates a one-sided surface: draw a line down the middle, and you'll return to the start without crossing an edge. This shows it's a one-sided surface. Similarly, if you trace the edge of the strip with your finger, you'll come back to where you started without ever lifting your finger or jumping edges.

[305] Knight and Butler, 197-198.

[306] Knight and Butler, 25, 221.

307 Knight and Butler, 225.

308 Knight and Butler, 225.

309 Knight and Butler, 157-166.

310 Knight and Butler, 175, 183-186.

311 Knight and Butler, 179.

312 A.J. Gentile. *The Why Files.* "The Moon Revealed: It's a Hollow Spaceship, so Who Built it and Why?" YouTube. 4 Aug. 2022. Retrieved: https://www.youtube.com/watch?v=laXhTcko-lg&t=11s. Abbr. Gentile, Moon Revealed.

313 Gentile, Moon Revealed.

314 Stroud, 47.

315 Stroud, 47. Stroud overlooks the crucial scientific concept of "space weathering" in understanding lunar dust. Without an atmosphere, the Moon's surface is constantly bombarded by micrometeorites and solar particles. As a result, surface dust is older in exposure age than deeper layers. See Yun-Zhao Wu et al. "Space Weathering of the Moon from *In Situ* Detection." *Research in Astronomy and Astrophysics*, vol. 19, no. 4, 2019, p. 051. *IOPscience*. Retrieved: https://iopscience.iop.org/article/10.1088/1674-4527/19/4/51/pdf.

316 Knight and Butler, 57, 67, 249.

317 Gentile, Moon Revealed.

318 Gentile, Moon Revealed.

319 Gentile, Moon Revealed.

320 Gentile, Moon Revealed.

321 Gentile, Moon Revealed.

322 Gentile, Moon Revealed.

323 Gentile, Moon Revealed.

324 Gentile, Moon Revealed.

325 Gentile, Moon Revealed.

326 Gentile, Moon Revealed.

327 Gentile, Moon Revealed.

328 Gentile, Moon Revealed.

329 Gentile, Mood Revealed.

330 Gentile, Moon Revealed.

331 Gentile, Moon Revealed.

332 Gentile, Moon Revealed.

333 Gentile, Moon Revealed.

334 Mikhail Vasin and Alexander Shcherbakov. "Is the Moon the Creation of Intelligence?" *Sputnik*, July 1970. Retrieved: https://www.scribd.com/document/33616146/Is-the-Moon-the-Creation-of-Intelligence. Abbr. Vasin and Shcherbakov.

335 Vasin and Shcherbakov.

336 Vasin and Shcherbakov.

337 Vasin and Shcherbakov.

338 Vasin and Shcherbakov.

339 Vasin and Shcherbakov.

340 Vasin and Shcherbakov.

341 Neil deGrasse Tyson, *To Infinity and Beyond: A Journey of Cosmic Discovery.* National Geographic, 2023, p. 116. Abbr. Tyson, Infinity.

342 Tyson, Infinity, 120.

343 Dr. Steven M. Greer, *Unacknowledged: An Exposé of the World's Greatest Secret.* A&M Publishing, L.L.C., 2017, p. 198. Abbr. Greer, Unacknowledged.

344 A.J. Gentile, *The Why Files,* "The Dark Side of the Moon | Alien Activity and the NASA Cover-Up," YouTube. 13 June 2024. Retrieved: https://www.youtube.com/watch?v=WqHimq-PT_s. Abbr. Gentile, Dark Side of the Moon.

345 Gentile, Dark Side of the Moon.

346 Gentile, Dark Side of the Moon.
347 Gentile, Dark Side of the Moon.
348 Gentile, Dark Side of the Moon.
349 Gentile, Dark Side of the Moon.
350 Greer, Unacknowledged, 202; Gentile, Dark Side of the Moon.
351 Gentile, Dark Side of the Moon.
352 Gentile, Dark Side of the Moon.
353 Gentile, Dark Side of the Moon.
354 Gentile, Dark Side of the Moon.
355 Gentile, Dark Side of the Moon.
356 Gentile, Dark Side of the Moon.
357 Greer, Unacknowledged, 198-199.
358 *Extreme Mysteries,* "UFO History & Origins | Citizen Hearing on UFO Disclosure | (Session 1)," YouTube. 18 May 2023. Retrieved: https://www.youtube.com/watch?v=249RG52UTBE. Timestamp 3:46-5:11.
359 Greer, Unacknowledged, 199.
360 Gentile, Dark Side of the Moon.
361 Greer, Unacknowledged, 204.
362 Greer, Unacknowledged, 205.
363 Gentile, Dark Side of the Moon.
364 Gentile, Dark Side of the Moon.
365 Gentile, Dark Side of the Moon.
366 Greer, Unacknowledged, 206.
367 Greer, Unacknowledged, 206.
368 Greer, Unacknowledged, 207.
369 Greer, Unacknowledged, 207.
370 Greer, Unacknowledged, 207.
371 Gentile, Dark Side of the Moon.
372 Gentile, Dark Side of the Moon.
373 Greer, Unacknowledged, 200.
374 Greer, Unacknowledged, 199.
375 Greer, Unacknowledged, 200.
376 Greer, Unacknowledged, xv, 201.
377 Reference unknown.
378 Voyager – NASA Science. Retrieved: https://science.nasa.gov/mission/voyager. Abbr. Voyager.
379 Charlie T. Finch, Todd J. Henry, et al. "The Solar Neighborhood XVIII." *The Astronomical Journal,* 133:2898-2907, 2007 June. Retrieved: https://www.astro.gsu.edu/~thenry/RECONS/published18.pdf. Abbr. Finch and Henry.
380 To estimate the time required for Voyager 1 to reach Gliese 445, the distance to the star (17.6 light-years) and the spacecraft's speed (10.5 miles per second) must be known. If Gliese 445 were not moving toward the Solar System, the travel time would be approximately 310,000 years. Because the star is moving closer, the relative closing speed reduces the time required for closest approach to approximately 41,600 years.
381 Voyager.
382 Voyager 1 – Interplanetary Mission. Retrieved: https://www.jpl.nasa.gov/missions/voyager-1. Abbr. Voyager 1.
383 Voyager; Voyager 1.
384 Voyager; Voyager 1.
385 What is the Deep Space Network? Retrieved: https://www.nasa.gov/directorates/somd/space-communications-navigation-program/what-is-the-deep-space-network.

386 Voyager; Voyager 1.

387 Carl Sagan and Frank D. Drake, *Murmurs of Earth: The Voyager Interstellar Record,* Random House, 1978.

388 Instructions for Aliens – NASA. Retrieved: https://www.nasa.gov/image-article/instructions-for-aliens.

389 Voyager; Voyager 1.

390 Meet Rasalhague, the Star with the Snake – *Sky & Telescope.* Retrieved: https://skyandtelescope.org/astronomy-news/meet-rasalhague-the-star-with-the-snake.

391 Barnard's Star Has a Confirmed Planet—At Last! – *Sky & Telescope.* Retrieved: https://skyandtelescope.org/astronomy-news/barnards-star-has-a-confirmed-planet-at-last.

392 João Alves, et al. "Dust Extinction and Molecular Cloud Structure: L977." *The Astrophysical Journal,* 506:292-305, 1998 October. Retrieved: https://iopscience.iop.org/article/10.1086/306243/pdf.

393 Charles J. Lada, et al. "The Nature of the Dense Core Population in the Pipe Nebula: Thermal Cores Under Pressure." *The Astrophysical Journal,* 672:410-422, 2008 January. Retrieved: https://iopscience.iop.org/article/10.1086/523837/pdf.

394 Ophiuchus Constellation – Messier Objects. Retrieved: https://www.messier-objects.com/tag/ophiuchus-constellation.

395 R.D. Jeffries, et al. "A revised age greater than 50 Myr for the young cluster IC 4665." *Monthly Notices of the Royal Astronomical Society,* 526(1), 1260-1267, 2023 November. The authors argue that IC 4665 is 55±3 million years old, older than earlier estimates. Retrieved: https://academic.oup.com/mnras/article/526/1/1260/7276635.

396 S. Giacintucci, et al. "Ophiuchus Galaxy Cluster: Record-Breaking Explosion by Black Hole Spotted." arXiv:2002.01291 [astro-ph.GA] 2020 February. Retrieved: https://www.chandra.harvard.edu/photo/2020/ophiuchus.

397 "10 Things You Might Not Know About Voyager's Famous 'Pale Blue Dot' Photo." *NASA Science.* Retrieved: https://science.nasa.gov/earth/10-things-you-might-not-know-about-voyagers-famous-pale-blue-dot-photo.

398 "NASA's Voyager 1 Spacecraft Breaks Into Interstellar Space." NASA, 2012. Retrieved: https://www.nasa.gov/mission_pages/voyager/voyager20120912.html.

399 "Voyager 1 and 2: The Interstellar Journal." NASA Jet Propulsion Laboratory, 2023. Retrieved: https://www.jpl.nasa.gov/missions/voyager.

400 Robert Wise, *Star Trek: The Motion Picture* (1979). Script. Retrieved: https://www.scripts.com/script-pdf-body.php?id=531. Abbr. The Motion Picture, script.

401 The Motion Picture, script.

402 "Star Trek and the Voyager 6 Connection." StarTrek.com, 2021. Retrieved: https://www.startrek.com.

403 "Voyager 1: NASA's Most Distant Spacecraft." NASA, 2023. Retrieved: https://www.nasa.gov/mission_pages/voyager/index.html.

404 The Motion Picture, script.

405 The History Channel, "Were Earth's First Stories About Alien Visitors?" *Ancient Aliens.* YouTube. 17 Sept. 2025. Retrieved: https://www.youtube.com/watch?v=OgxNfLMej5w. Abbr. History, First Stories.

406 History, First Stories.

407 History, First Stories.

408 History, First Stories.

409 History, First Stories.

410 History, First Stories.

411 History, First Stories.

412 History, First Stories.

413 History, First Stories.

414 History, First Stories.

415 History, First Stories.

416 History, First Stories.

417 The History Channel. "Evidence of Early Alien Contact with Earth." *Ancient Aliens.* YouTube, 16 Nov. 2024. Retrieved: https://www.youtube.com/watch?v=UfPz00kHFyY. Abbr. History, Early Alien Contact.

418 History, Early Alien Contact.

419 Von Däniken, Chariots, 45-48.

420 Ezekiel 1:4-5, 15-19. *The New Catholic Study Bible, St. Jerome Edition.* Thomas Nelson Publishers, 1985, p. 685.

421 Erich von Däniken. "Ezekiel's Wheel." *Ancient Aliens: The Official Companion Book,* by Kevin Burns, HarperElixir, 2016, p. 2. Abbr. Von Däniken, Ezekiel's Wheel.

422 Von Däniken, Ezekiel's Wheel, 3.

423 History, Early Alien Contact.

424 History, Early Alien Contact.

425 Ezekiel 8:3, 40:1ff.

426 Von Däniken, Ezekiel's Wheel, 7-9.

427 History, Early Alien Contact.

428 History, Early Alien Contact.

429 History, Early Alien Contact.

430 History, Early Alien Contact.

431 History, Early Alien Contact.

432 History, Early Alien Contact.

433 History, Early Alien Contact.

434 History, Early Alien Contact.

435 History, Early Alien Contact.

436 History, Early Alien Contact.

437 History, Early Alien Contact.

438 History, Early Alien Contact.

439 David Hatcher Childress. "Temples of Blood and Gold." *Ancient Aliens: The Official Companion Book,* by Kevin Burns, HarperElixir, 2016, pp. 76-77.

440 History, Early Alien Contact.

441 History, Early Alien Contact.

442 History, Early Alien Contact.

443 History, Early Alien Contact.

444 *Real Life Lore.* "What's Hidden Under the Ice of Antarctica?" YouTube, 12, July 2024. Retrieved: https://www.youtube.com/watch?v=KOnB47PyZJw. Abbr. Real Life Lore.

445 Real Life Lore.

446 Real Life Lore.

447 Real Life Lore.

448 Real Life Lore.

449 Real Life Lore.

450 The History Channel, "Secret Pyramids Hide Beneath Earth's Surface." *Ancient Aliens: Declassified.* YouTube, 26 Oct. 2024. Retrieved: https://www.youtube.com/watch?v=JlIQP60FAO0. Abbr. History, Secret Pyramids.

451 History, Early Alien Contact.

452 History, Early Alien Contact.

453 History, Early Alien Contact.

454 History, Early Alien Contact.

455 Giorgio A. Tsoukalos. "The Egyptian Connection." *Ancient Aliens: The Official Companion Book,* by Kevin Burns, HarperElixir, 2016, p. 12. Abbr. Tsoukalos, Egyptian Connection. Note: Tsoukalos's article prints "every ninety seconds," but this is likely a typo or miscalculation, as

the commonly circulated figure in *Ancient Aliens* episodes and related commentary is "every nine seconds."

456 Tsoukalos, Egyptian Connection, 12.
457 Tsoukalos, Egyptian Connection, 12.
458 Tsoukalos, Egyptian Connection, 16.
459 Tsoukalos, Egyptian Connection, 17.
460 Tsoukalos, Egyptian Connection, 14-15.
461 Tsoukalos, Egyptian Connection, 18.
462 Tsoukalos, Egyptian Connection, 14.
463 Tsoukalos, Egyptian Connection, 14.
464 Tsoukalos, Egyptian Connection, 15.
465 Tsoukalos, Egyptian Connection, 22.
466 Tsoukalos, Egyptian Connection, 22.
467 Tsoukalos, Egyptian Connection, 22.
468 Tsoukalos, Egyptian Connection, 22.
469 History, Secret Pyramids.
470 History, Secret Pyramids.
471 History, Secret Pyramids.
472 History, Secret Pyramids.
473 History, Secret Pyramids.
474 History, Secret Pyramids.
475 History, Secret Pyramids.
476 History, Secret Pyramids.
477 History, Secret Pyramids.
478 History, Secret Pyramids.
479 Giorgio A. Tsoukalos. "The Great Puzzle of Puma Punku." *Ancient Aliens: The Official Companion Book,* by Kevin Burns, HarperElixir, 2016, pp. 48-50. Abbr. Tsoukalos, Puma Punku.
480 Tsoukalos, Puma Punku, 50-51.
481 Tsoukalos, Puma Punku, 51.
482 Tsoukalos, Puma Punku, 53.
483 Tsoukalos, Puma Punku, 53.
484 Tsoukalos, Puma Punku, 53.
485 Tsoukalos, Puma Punku, 53-54.
486 Tsoukalos, Puma Punku, 54.
487 Tsoukalos, Puma Punku, 54.
488 Tsoukalos, Puma Punku, 55-56.
489 Tsoukalos, Puma Punku, 56.
490 Tsoukalos, Puma Punku, 57.
491 Tsoukalos, Puma Punku, 57.
492 Firestone, 2. Earth's history shows recurring mass extinctions from natural catastrophes. Richard Firestone proposes that a comet impact 12,900 years ago triggered the Younger Dryas, part of a cosmic debris cycle, suggesting that we are currently living in the sixth extinction within this cycle. Other theories point to stellar or galactic causes, while ancient-astronaut ideas propose alien "resets" of civilization. Today, humanity is driving a new, self-made extinction through climate change, overpopulation, habitat loss, and pollution.
493 Steven M. Greer, M.D., *Disclosure: Military and Government Witnesses Reveal the Greatest Secrets in Modern History,* 2001, p. 5. Abbr. Greer, Disclosure.
494 Greer, Disclosure, 22.
495 Greer, Disclosure, 21.
496 Greer, Disclosure, 13.
497 Greer, Disclosure, 14.

498 Greer, Disclosure, 14.

499 Greer, Disclosure, 14. His emphasis.

500 See below in the main text on the evolution of terminology used to describe UFOs and the rationale behind these shifts (Section 17: *The ODNI Report and the New Terminology*).

501 Greer, Disclosure, 112-128.

502 Greer, Disclosure, 113-115.

503 Greer, Disclosure, 256.

504 Greer, Disclosure, 256.

505 Greer, Disclosure, 255-256.

506 Greer, Disclosure, 257-261.

507 Greer, Disclosure, 328-329.

508 Greer, Disclosure, 326-328.

509 Greer, Disclosure, 325.

510 Greer, Disclosure, 325.

511 Greer, Disclosure, 330.

512 Greer, Disclosure, 332-333.

513 Greer, Disclosure, 329.

514 Greer, Disclosure, 329.

515 Greer, Disclosure, 330.

516 Greer, Disclosure, 330.

517 Greer, Disclosure, 331.

518 Greer, Disclosure, 338.

519 Greer, Disclosure, 332; Unacknowledged, 168.

520 Greer, Disclosure, 332; Unacknowledged, 168.

521 Greer, Disclosure, 332; Unacknowledged, 168.

522 Greer, Disclosure, 332; Unacknowledged, 168.

523 Greer, Disclosure, 14.

524 Greer, Disclosure, 15.

525 Greer, Disclosure, 16.

526 Greer, Disclosure, 17.

527 Greer, Disclosure, 17.

528 Office of the Director of National Intelligence. *Preliminary Assessment: Unidentified Aerial Phenomena*. 25 June 2021. Retrieved: https://www.dni.gov/files/ODNI/documents/assessments/Prelimary-Assessment-UAP-20210625.pdf. Abbr. ODNI, Preliminary Assessment.

529 ODNI, Preliminary Assessment.

530 Neil deGrasse Tyson. *StarTalk.* "Breaking Down UAP Footage with the Head of The Pentagon's UAP Taskforce, Dr. Jon Kosloski." YouTube, 12 Aug 2025. Retrieved: https://www.youtube.com/watch?v=mvsU4p0Gsas&t=862s. Abbr. Tyson, StarTalk.

531 Tyson, StarTalk.

532 Tyson, StarTalk.

533 Tyson, StarTalk.

534 Greer, Unacknowledged, xiii-xiv.

535 Greer, Unacknowledged, 63-64.

536 Greer, Unacknowledged, 63-64.

537 Greer, Unacknowledged, 66.

538 Greer, Unacknowledged, 66.

539 A.J. Gentile, *The Why Files,* "Killer Patents & Secret Science Vol. 1 | Free Energy & Anti-Gravity Cover-Ups." YouTube. 19 April 2024. Retrieved: https://www.youtube.com/watch?v=-ZRwlYtAMps&t=2553s.

540 Greer, Unacknowledged, 66.

541 Greer, Unacknowledged, 66-67.

542 Greer, Unacknowledged, 67.

543 Greer, Unacknowledged, 67.

544 Greer, Unacknowledged, 68. His emphasis.

545 Greer, Unacknowledged, 68, 281ff.

546 Greer, Unacknowledged, 284-285.

547 *Extreme Mysteries,* "UFOs - Truth, Lies & Coverup (Session 4) | The Citizen Hearing on UFO Disclosure," June 21, 2023. Retrieved:
https://www.youtube.com/watch?v=DCiOm7EV5wA. Timestamp 20:30-24:21. Abbr. Citizen Hearing, Session 4.

548 Citizen Hearing, Session 4.

549 Citizen Hearing, Session 4.

550 Citizen Hearing, Session 4.

551 Citizen Hearing, Session 4.

552 Citizen Hearing, Session 4.

553 Citizen Hearing, Session 4.

554 Citizen Hearing, Session 4.

555 Greer, Unacknowledged, 161.

556 Greer, Unacknowledged, 161.

557 Greer, Unacknowledged, 166, 168.

558 Greer, Unacknowledged, 83-84.

559 Greer, Unacknowledged, 75-76.

560 Greer, Unacknowledged, 76.

561 Greer, Unacknowledged, 6, 75-98.

562 Greer, Unacknowledged, 161-162.

563 Greer, Unacknowledged, 162.

564 Greer, Unacknowledged, 175-196.

565 Greer, Unacknowledged, 175.

566 Greer, Unacknowledged, 11.

567 Greer, Unacknowledged, 11.

568 Greer, Unacknowledged, 12-13.

569 Greer, Unacknowledged, 12.

570 Greer, Unacknowledged, 12.

571 Greer, Unacknowledged, 12.

572 Greer, Unacknowledged, 175-176.

573 Greer, Unacknowledged, 176-177.

574 Nietzsche, *Ecce Homo* (1888). Translated by R.J. Hollingdale with an Introduction by Michael Tanner. Penguin Books, 1992. Foreword (Sec. 3), p. 4.

575 Nietzsche, *The Gay Science* (1882). Translated by Walter Kaufmann. Vintage Books, 1974, (Sections. 343 and 382), pp. 280 and 346.

www.ingramcontent.com/pod-product-compliance
Lightning Source LLC
Chambersburg PA
CBHW051834150726
47998CB00001B/421